FOUR H

a pl
by

TERENCE BRADY
&
CHARLOTTE BINGHAM

ACT ONE

SCENE ONE. THE LIVING ROOM IN JIMMY AND VIC'S HOUSE.
EVENING

The house is a village house in the West Country. The
sitting room is furnished comfortably with old furniture,
mostly brown. Notably there is a fine old Queen Anne card
table set with antique chairs for the bridge game that is
in progress, there is a good Victorian sideboard on which
rests an un-ornamented silver vase in which flowers are
arranged. There are some good paintings and drawings on
the walls, none notably so, more the collection of people
who have bought what has taken their fancy. On one wall a
larger painting is missing, notable by the pale coloured
rectangular mark the missing work has left behind. There
is also perhaps a fine but old small Persian rug on the
floor lying on top of the carpet beneath. It is a winter
evening in January so the curtains are drawn.

There is as noted a bridge game is in progress. The four
players are JIMMY and his wife VIC, HUGH and the widow
ISOBEL. HUGH, partnered with ISOBEL is dummy. There is
complete silence as ISOBEL plays the hand. JIMMY and VIC
stare intently at their own hands, each in their own
fashion.

HUGH gets up from his chair and stretches. He walks round
the table and looks over ISOBEL'S shoulder at her hand.
JIMMY at once holds his cards tight to his chest as does
VIC. Finally, after an interminable wait, ISOBEL seems
about to play the card she has slowly selected from her
hand. JIMMY eyes VIC hopefully. HUGH sees what his
partner is about to play. He says and shows nothing.
ISOBEL looks up at him equally blank faced. HUGH goes
back to his side of the table and takes his drink from a
smaller table set nearby. He sits glass in hand and takes
a slow sip. ISOBEL frowns at the card she was about to
play then slowly pushes it back down into her hand. JIMMY

glances at VIC who raises her eyebrows to him privately. ISOBEL leans across the table and resets dummy's hand nearer her. HUGH helps her. She doesn't look at him, just at dummy. Then back at her hand. Then back at dummy. She inhales slowly then exhales, equally slowly. VIC looks at JIMMY who raises one eyebrow back to her. ISOBEL stares at dummy and shakes her head. She screws her eyes up tightly shut and stares blindly up at the ceiling.

JIMMY clears his throat. VIC makes two strange little kissing noises by pursing her lips together. ISOBEL frowns at her. VIC smiles back at her. Isobel frowns even more deeply. She draws a card from her hand, probably the same card she was going to play first. All wait for the play. ISOBEL finally rejects the play and returns the card to her hand. JIMMY shuts his eyes slowly. HUGH stares into his drink. VIC'S frown deepens. JIMMY starts a little finger drumming on the table. ISOBEL glares at him. JIMMY slowly stops.

Finally after giving a deep sigh of committal, ISOBEL plays a card. JIMMY plays a card, ISOBEL drums her fingers herself as she regards dummy's hand, goes to play one, thinks better of it, stops, regards dummy again, then nods to herself once in reassurance and plays the card she had first rejected. VIC eyes her, then produces the winning card from her hand and wins the trick. JIMMY collects the four cards VIC pushes at him across the table and taps them neatly into a trick. VIC is already playing her card for the next trick. Seeing it, ISOBEL is visibly wrong footed for the second time. She stares at VIC who smiles sweetly back at her. ISOBEL ponders, then plays. JIMMY plays his card and seeing there is nothing she can do, ISOBEL plays from dummy. JIMMY picks up the winning trick, taps the cards neatly into perfect order and adds the second trick to his pile. He then plays again, without expression. ISOBEL stares with ill-concealed horror at what she sees is happening. HUGH, frowns slightly and slowly put his hands on top of his head.

ISOBEL looks at JIMMY who raises his eyebrows to her. ISOBEL takes deep breath, plays from dummy, for VIC quickly to produce another winning card for the third trick. She pushes the four cards at JIMMY who does his collection routine, while VIC taps the fresh card she has just played with one indicative forefinger. ISOBEL glances at her and plays what she knows is another losing card. JIMMY wins the trick and gathers. HUGH sticks his hands straight up into the air and pulls a face of slight stupefaction. ISOBEL'S face is now pretty rigid. JIMMY leads again, and again VIC produces a winner. HUGH puts his hands back down on to the top of his head and smiles weakly at ISOBEL who blanks him. ISOBEL loses again. HUGH breathes in, rises and pours himself another drink. He returns to staring out of the window. ISOBEL plays. She wins this trick and the next. The speed of her play accelerates as she wins another trick, but now she's playing too fast and thinking she has won the trick is about to collect when JIMMY produces another surprise from his hand - ISOBEL obviously having miscounted trumps - and picks up the winning trick.

HUGH does his best to keep a brave face as ISOBEL tries valiantly to salvage what she can, but disaster has struck which she realises as the hand finishes. There is a long silence during which looks are exchanged, knuckles, crunched, yawns are yawned, and stretches are stretched while ISOBEL stares blankly down at the table.

                    ISOBEL
How stupid can you be -

                    JIMMY
You don't want an answer to that -

                    HUGH
What's the damage?

                    VIC
Four short.

                    HUGH
Ah well.

                    VIC
              (scoring)
Four light - doubled -

                    JIMMY
And pregnant.

                    ISOBEL
              (barely audibly)
Sorry, partner.

                    JIMMY
              (writing down score)
Which is one thousand one hundred points to us -

                    VIC
              (to ISOBEL)
It is the first time you've played together.

                    ISOBEL
We should never have been in four spades.

JIMMY
How many points did you have, petal?

ISOBEL
Enough to open.

HUGH
And I had enough to respond. I had nine.

ISOBEL
And I had - about twelve.

JIMMY and VIC exchange a look.

JIMMY
(to ISOBEL)
No wonder you went four light.

VIC
(warning)
Jimmy?

HUGH
We had twenty one points.

JIMMY
And went four light.

ISOBEL
We shouldn't have been in four spades. My fault.

She stares down at the table for a moment, then up at the ceiling.

ISOBEL
(cont'd)
Excuse me -

Isobel rises and hurries from the room. ALL stare after her.

VIC
(angry/to JIMMY)
No post-mortems, remember? You can see she's still all over the shop.

JIMMY
We're playing bridge. Not beggar your neighbour.

VIC shakes her head as she gathers up the tricks and discards and hands them to JIMMY to make.

VIC
And I said it were too soon.

JIMMY
This was your idea. Not mine.

HUGH
Look. It doesn't matter. Win or lose. It doesn't matter. But under the circumstances I do think no post-mortems is a good idea.

JIMMY
(collecting the cards)
If my partner had just gone four light doubled and vulnerable I wouldn't be happy with just a post-mortem - I'd want a full scale public enquiry.

VIC
Very funny I'm sure. Anyhow. Anyhow as I meant to say earlier but never got the chance - fancy the two of you knowing each other. You and Isobel.

HUGH
I grew up round here. As did Isobel.

VIC
So what brought you back?

HUGH
My father died and left me the house. The family house.

VIC
I see. So - so you're back to where you started.

HUGH
Absolutely. I was born here. I got married from here. And now probably this is where I shall hand in my dinner plate.

VIC
How come you got married from here?

HUGH
(cutting in)
Mary's my second wife. We were only married three years ago.

VIC
Right. Got it.

HUGH
My first wife Catherine - we got divorced.

JIMMY
You shouldn't have got divorced. You should have gone for a legal separation. Gives you time to hide your money.

VIC
You just go and see if Isobel's okay, all right?

JIMMY
You go. This was your bright idea, Mavis.

VIC
Did you know Tom, Hugh? Isobel's — No. I don't suppose you did.

HUGH
No I didn't know Tom. In fact this is the first time I've seen Isobel since we — since goodness knows when.

VIC
Tom was a really nice bloke. He and Isobel were devoted. He just adored Isobel.

JIMMY
Someone should really go and see if she's all right. It's her deal.

VIC
You can deal for her. Cut to him, Hugh.
            (to JIMMY)
And you should have listened to mother.

JIMMY
You were the one who did the inviting.

VIC
I was only trying to do the right thing.

JIMMY
I've been wondering what to put on your headstone.

VIC
Very droll I don't think.

JIMMY
I was only trying to do the right thing.

VIC
I know what I'm going to put on yours. *Despite his claims he was not immortal.*

JIMMY
Wait and see. You just wait and see.

                        VIC
Sorry about this, Hugh. But then - you know. It hasn't
been long. I mean it's been hardly not three month. Since
Tom. You knows. Since Tom -
            (silence)
Since Tom -

                        JIMMY
Died. Which as some would have it is a mite too soon to
expect the widow to make merry.

                        VIC
I was thinking of Isobel.

                        JIMMY
She was gagging for a game of bridge.

                        VIC
That's nice. That really is.

                        JIMMY
You were, pet. You were getting withdrawal symptoms.
            (singing)
You were bidding in your sleep -

                        VIC
Sometimes you are about as funny as one of them so called
stand up comedians.
            (noticing ISOBEL'S return)
And will you just listen to that rain. Will it never stop
raining?

                        JIMMY
You were gagging for a game.

                        VIC
I have never known such a *wet winter.*

VIC has managed to draw JIMMY'S attention to ISOBEL'S
RETURN. HUGH stands up. ISOBEL still has her hankie to
her nose which she gives a light blow then puts the
hankie in her sleeve.

                        ISOBEL
Right. Good. So where were we? It was my deal, I think.

                        VIC
Jimmy's dealt for you, duck. It's all right.

                        ISOBEL
Oh. Right. Right thank you, Jimmy. That was very kind.
Thank you.

ISOBEL sits back at the table and they all pick up their cards and sort them.

JIMMY
Right. So when you're ready - it's you to bid.

ISOBEL
(still sorting her cards)
Sorry about that last hand, partner.

HUGH
No need. It's only a game, partner. It's just a game.

ISOBEL is still sorting her cards. She glances across at HUGH then continues with her sorting.

JIMMY
(to ISOBEL)
Still you to bid, pet.

ISOBEL
Yes. I know. Sorry. Whose bid what so far?

JIMMY
Nobody's bid nothing, petal. Because you dealt.

ISOBEL
I thought someone just said you dealt.

JIMMY
I dealt - for you.

ISOBEL
Oh yes. Yes of course. Sorry. So in that case it's me to bid.

JIMMY
She's got it. I do believe she's got it.

VIC
(glaring at JIMMY)
You take your time, sweetheart. You just take your time.

JIMMY
Yes. Why don't you do that. And don't worry about it. We're not doing anything all month.

ISOBEL
It's just after that last hand….
(silence)
Oh Lord.
(silence)
Two clubs.

JIMMY

No bid.

HUGH
(regarding his hand)

Three hearts.

VIC

No.

ISOBEL
(after a moment)

Four no trumps.

JIMMY

No.

HUGH

Five hearts.

VIC

No bid.

ISOBEL

Five no trump.

JIMMY

No bid.

HUGH

Six clubs.

VIC

No.

ISOBEL
(pause)

Six hearts.

Silence.

JIMMY

Double.

HUGH

No.

VIC

No.

ISOBEL
(thoughtfully)

Redouble.

HUGH stares at her. ISOBEL smiles back weakly.

JIMMY
No bid.

HUGH
No.

VIC
No bid - and they're Hugh's hearts.

HUGH
(staring at his hand, engrossed)
Yes. Right. Right.

After a moment, after play has begun, ISOBEL gets up and starts to wander round the room. The three at the table start to play the hand in silence. ISOBEL finally stops in front of a mark on the wall where a painting recently hung.

ISOBEL
The Woman in the Hat's gone.

SILENCE from the players who are engrossed in the hand.

ISOBEL
What happened to the painting of the Woman in the Hat. The woman with the funny hand?

VIC
Your partner is trying to make a rather tricky small slam, pet.

ISOBEL
Yes of course. Sorry, partner.

VIC
Doubled.

JIMMY
And redoubled.

ISOBEL comes over to the table to spectate. She stands by HUGH'S shoulder. She frowns when she sees his hand.

HUGH
I would rather you didn't stand there, Isobel - if you don't mind.

ISOBEL
Sorry. Wasn't thinking. Sorry.

HUGH
It's the old concentration.

VIC
(automatically)
Less of the old.

HUGH
The concentration is not all that it used to be.

ISOBEL
You should try taking magnesium. Magnesium's very good for concentration. And for the memory. At least I think it's magnesium.

The THREE play on. It's hard going for HUGH. ISOBEL walks round the table and stands well back behind JIMMY but still peers at his hand.

ISOBEL
Someone recommended magnesium to me a couple of months ago. Since when I haven't wondered once what I was doing in the larder.

Her eyes slowly widen as she sees what's in JIMMY'S hand. She blinks then returns to stare at the painting in silence.

HUGH
(as he loses a trick)
Blast. Blast, blow and dammit.

JIMMY
Language.

ISOBEL looks at HUGH, then returns to stare briefly where the painting hung.

ISOBEL
The Lady in the Hat. You thought it might be by someone quite famous, didn't you? What's happened to her?

VIC
Later, duchess - if you don't mind.
(to HUGH)
Hard luck, pet.
(as she takes the trick)

HUGH
I thought your partner had the Queen.

ISOBEL
We're not going down again, are we, partner?

HUGH
Fraid so. Queen in the wrong place. Rest are mine.
(putting down his cards)

ISOBEL
(comes to peer at the damage)
I had twenty six points.

HUGH
We'd have made it if the Queen of trumps had been the other side.

VIC
(scoring)
Another four hundred points to us.

HUGH
Don't worry, partner. Early doors.

VIC
For the life of me I still don't know what that means. Early *doors?*

JIMMY'S turn to deal while VIC makes the second pack.

HUGH
Something to do with football they tell me. Early doors.

ISOBEL
I thought we were home and whatevered. Hosed.
(to HUGH)
How many points did you have?

HUGH
It was the distribution. Not the points. Nothing wrong with the bidding.

VIC
The Lady in the Hat has gone to be valued, if you're still interested.

ISOBEL
Really? Oh. Why? Not that it's any of my business.

JIMMY
The daughter has taken it off to be valued.

ISOBEL
Annie?

VIC
Jimmy –

JIMMY
Annie's taken it off to London.

VIC
That's quite enough.

JIMMY
It's been taken off to London and the same thing will happen to it as happened to the silver bon-bon dishes.

ISOBEL
Yes. Yes I remember the dishes. Annie took those off to be valued as well.

VIC
Annie took them off to be re-silvered.

JIMMY
They were last seen on *Going For a Song*.

VIC
Stop being so daft.

JIMMY
Right. And since proceedings have come to a bit of a halt, why don't I get us all a drink?
          (rising)
All together now, I don't mind if I do.

VIC
I put some nibbles out on the side there, Jimmy. In those bowls. As it happens I could do with stretching the legs.
          (standing and adjusting her
          dress)
Annie sent me some of this new so called *control* underwear. Meant to give you a bum like a Duchess' sister. Fat chance.
          (as she adjusts herself)
Bloody things are cutting me throat.

JIMMY
          (at the drinks)
Right? Same as same as? Right.

VIC
Tell you something else the daughter recommended. Them alarm things. The ones you hang round your neck? You know.

ISOBEL
Not so. Those are for old people, Vic. I mean *old* old people. Not people like you and Jimmy.

VIC
Annie's no spring chicken herself, you know. She'll be forty something next month And she's still dressing like a Spice girl.

ISOBEL
You want to be very careful before you go getting one of those alarms things, Vic. Or you could end up like that poor woman who slipped on her stairs, got the cord of her alarm tangled round the bannister and very nearly strangled herself.

VIC
I say. Really? Did the alarm go off?

ISOBEL
I suppose it must have done. Otherwise she wouldn't have been on Breakfast television.

VIC
We don't bother with Breakfast TV anymore. It's nothing but weather. Weather, weather, weather.

JIMMY
You mean wither. The wither belongs to Jockland. Don't you just love the Jocks? They want oot from the UK - until it comes to captaining the Ryder Cup.
(holds up bottle to HUGH)

HUGH
Nothing for me. I'm driving.

JIMMY
Right. And as the man said - don't drink and drive. Don't even putt.

HUGH
Too right.

JIMMY
(pouring himself a drink)
The man who also said you're not really drunk unless you're hanging on to the floor. Fair Isobella?

ISOBEL
No thanks Jimmy. I'm driving as well. Something else I'm going to have to get used to. Driving everywhere. Because of course I've never been the best of drivers. But there you are. Needs must.

                    VIC
It all takes time, pet.

                    JIMMY
It takes time to ruin a world - but time is all it takes.

Silence.

                    HUGH
If you don't feel like driving yourself home tonight,
Isobel -

                    ISOBEL
No I'll be fine, Hugh. Really.

                    JIMMY
Ice. We are in dire need of ice.

JIMMY goes.

                    ISOBEL
          (beat)
Is Jimmy all right?

                    VIC
Shouldn't he be?

                    ISOBEL
It's nothing. It's just I thought the shape of his face
had changed. It's probably nothing.

                    VIC
He's had his hair cut if that's what you're on about.
And it weren't the usual girl. The usual girl was off
sick - again. Pregnant. Again. Seems the smart thing
nowadays is have all your babies before you get married.

                    ISOBEL
Absolutely. We went to a wedding not so long ago where
the two daughters were the bridesmaids, the son was the
best man and the bride's train was carried by their
grand-children.

                    VIC
Can you imagine what our mums would have said.

                    ISOBEL
Both the bridesmaids were banged up. Tom said it was more
like a fertility rite than a wedding. Was Annie serious
about you getting those alarm things?

VIC
You bet. She can't wait to put us in one of them Don't Care Homes. Jimmy won't have it. He said he's buggered if he's going to end his days behind a wall of filing cabinets jammed in by a lot of illegal immigrants.

ISOBEL
I'm with Jimmy on that one.

JIMMY
(returning)
Ice anyone? As the Second Officer on the -

VIC
No thank you, Jimmy. No Titanic jokes tonight, thank you. It was bad enough watching the series.

JIMMY
I don't think I offered you a drink, fair Isabella. You really ought to slip out of those wet clothes and into a dry martini.

VIC
She told you, Jimmy - she's driving? And we all know what the man said about that, thank you.
(JIMMY goes)
Anyway, Isobel pet - to get back to this alarm business. Fact is I had took a bit of a tumble before Christmas. Hence the fuss. I slipped over on the front step and banged my head on the porch.

ISOBEL
That could have been nasty.

VIC
Course soon as Annie got wind of it we start getting these links to all these websites for all this stuff for us *old folk*. Things like Invisible hearing aids. They'd be a fat lot of good now, wouldn't they? Hello? Has anyone seen my invisible hearing aid? What does it look like? I don't know - it's invisible. And for baths with doors in them.

ISOBEL
I've often wondered how those things they work. Surely as soon as you open the door to get out the whole bathroom floods?

VIC
(glancing round)
Do you think Hugh's okay? He looks a bit beached.

                    ISOBEL
He's okay. I didn't know you knew Hugh.

                    VIC
I didn't know you knew Hugh either. And that's not easy
to say.

                    ISOBEL
We used to - we both grew up round here.

                    VIC
I got that.

                    ISOBEL
Everybody knew everybody round here. How did you meet
him?

                    VIC
Bridge. At the dreaded Colin and Marge's. Just after he
and his wife moved into The Old Milk House. Wife number
two apparently. Mary. Who Doesn't Play Bridge. So you
know. When we thought we might have a game this evening -
the three of us - I asked him if he'd care to play. He's
a good player. He's made up a four several times since -
since recently, you know.
            (beat/looks round to HUGH)
I hope he's all right. You all right there, Hugh?

HUGH is sitting at the cards table by himself, playing
patience, while JIMMY pours himself another drink.

                    HUGH
            (looking up)
Who? Me? Me I'm fine, thanks. Fine.

                    VIC
Good. And what's Mary doing tonight?
            (to ISOBEL)
Mary's always up to something or other.

                    HUGH
At some new class or other.

                    VIC
            (to ISOBEL)
Always out learning something new. What's the class for
this time, Hugh?

                    HUGH
Something known as bargello apparently. Which I always
thought was some sort of a medieval fortification.

ISOBEL
It's some form of needlework, isn't it?

VIC
Don't ask me. You're the teacher.

ISOBEL
Was the teacher. Yes I'm sure bargello's some sort of needlework. Sort of thing I've never had the time for.

VIC
Yes. Yes well now maybe – maybe you might just have. Now you have some time to yourself –

ISOBEL
I have quite a lot of time to myself actually.

VIC
So now might be a good time to find something with which to – to – well. To fill it. To fill all that time. You have to yourself.

ISOBEL
Like I said, bargello and I are not compatible.

VIC
There are all sorts of other things, pet. Another friend of ours. Another –

ISOBEL
(pause)
Widow?

VIC
(nods)
This other friend of ours Jenny – she's just started rambling.

JIMMY
Unlike you, beloved. You started rambling years ago.

VIC
Jenny has actually made a *lot* of new friends.

ISOBEL
I don't particularly like the great outdoors. I'm really quite agoraphobic. And I certainly don't do stiles.

                    VIC
There are other things, pet. Painting. A lot of people
take up painting. Or photography. Or what about jam? You
make *very* good jam, pet. Another friend of ours – another
recently bereaved friend – she got heavily into jam. In
just a small way at first. But then the whole thing took
off and now her preserves are in shops and supermarkets
everywhere. She even won a jam competition. Just like
that film. You know. You know the one.

                    ISOBEL
I'm not sure I do. I can't actually remembering sitting
through a film all about jam.

                    VIC
She had a baby – the actress. In this film. And she made
baby food! That was it. She made baby food. What the hell
was it called?

                    HUGH
Bringing Up Baby?

                    VIC
Bringing Up Baby?

                    HUGH
Maybe *Bringing Up Baby Food?*

                    VIC
Baby Boom. That was it. The film was called *Baby Boom.*

                    ISOBEL
I don't think I ever saw it. Not that I'd remember. The
other night I lay awake for hours trying to remember what
it's called when you can't remember anything.

                    VIC
The girl in the film had this baby and made her own baby
food – and got extremely rich.

                    ISOBEL
Fine. I see. So the plan is that now I have all this time
on my hands – the plan would be for me to have a baby and
start making baby food. Right?

                    VIC
No no no. No not exactly. I was thinking more along the
lines of jam actually.

                    ISOBEL
Do I still have to have a baby?

VIC
No of course not. Of course not. Not if you don't want to.

ISOBEL looks at her then smiles at VIC.

JIMMY
Come on, children. Back to the table.
(heading for the cards)

ISOBEL
Supposing The Lady in the Hat - supposing she is valuable.

VIC
No harm supposing, I suppose. And I suppose it would dig us out of a hole. It would mean we could stay here. It would mean we wouldn't have to down size to a shoe box, I suppose.

ISOBEL
I didn't realise there was a problem.

VIC
There isn't. Yet. Come on or Jimmy'll start foaming at the ears.

JIMMY
Come on, you two. And it's the fair Victoriana to deal.

VIC
(to ISOBEL/sitting)
So keep an eye on the old Antiques Road Show. You never know.

ISOBEL
I love the way everyone on those programmes has always been gifted these priceless little treasures by their grateful employers. They're forever finding bits of Jacobean silver in skips or being given Faberge jewels by the people whose ovens they've just been cleaning.

JIMMY starts to shuffle the second pack.

HUGH
I don't know about you, partner - but I have a feeling our luck is about to change.

ISOBEL cuts the pack for VIC to deal, and VIC starts to deal. Everyone picks up their cards except ISOBEL who has suddenly become suddenly distracted.

ISOBEL
I think I should go home actually. If no one minds.

VIC
Why, pet? Go home? Why- has something upset you?

ISOBEL
No - no I'm just suddenly finding it all a bit difficult. Sorry.

VIC
You don't have to go, you know. We can just - we could just stop playing - and you could just stay. You can stay here, pet.

ISOBEL
I can't, Vic. I can't *stay* here.

VIC
Why not? Mea casa and all that.

ISOBEL
I know - but sooner or later I'd have to go home and when I did I'd still have to go through exactly what I'm going through now all over again.

VIC
So just stay here tonight then.

ISOBEL
Staying here would only make things worse. Just as I hoped that coming here tonight might make things better.

VIC
I see. I am sorry, pet. Real sorry.

JIMMY
Couldn't we please just play this hand out?

VIC
No, Jimmy. We could not. Okay?

JIMMY
(regarding his hand)
If you could see what I got -

HUGH
Let me drive you home, Isobel.

ISOBEL
I'm all right. Really.

VIC
Hugh's right. Let him drive you.

ISOBEL
I really would rather drive myself. Really. Sorry.

VIC
At least - look at least give us a call. When you get home.

ISOBEL
Of course. Sorry. Goodnight everyone. And - sorry.

ISOBEL She goes. She stops by the door briefly, doesn't turn round, then finally leaves.

HUGH
I think perhaps I should follow her. Make sure she's all right.

JIMMY
Best left well alone, I'd say. For the time being.

VIC
I wonder what started it up? She was going great guns. We were going fine and then suddenly - I wonder what triggered it?

HUGH
Could be anything, I imagine. With what she's going through. It was very brave to come out in the first place.

VIC
And now she has to go back to an empty house. Doesn't bear thinking about. Going back to silence. To just an empty chair - and an empty bed. No talk, no laughter.
        (silence)
I can't imagine what it must be like.

HUGH
I think perhaps I should go as well.

JIMMY
        (ever hopeful)
You don't have to. We could play a three-hander. We could play cut-throat.

VIC
No I don't think so, Jimmy.

HUGH
Look - if there's anything I can do.

VIC
There's not anything any of us can do, love - nothing other than we're doing already.

HUGH
In that case I'll say Goodnight.

JIMMY
Night night.

VIC
Night, Hugh. Thanks for coming.

HUGH
I'll see myself out.
(goes)

VIC
(sitting at the card
table/after a moment)
Do you suppose she'll be all right?

JIMMY
As right as any of us are going to be. .

VIC
It's been hardly any time at all. I did say.
(seeing him sitting at the
table)
And now what are you doing?

JIMMY
(examining the other dealt
hands)
We might as well as see what we would have got.

VIC
Oh Jimmy.
(shakes her head)
Jimmy don't you ever think of anything else but bloody bridge?

JIMMY
Nope. Not much else bears thinking about.

He glances at her, picks up his cards, and starts slowly sorting through them. VIC looks at him and shakes her head slowly.

LIGHTS DOWN
MUSIC: Dave Brubeck piano/ *Thank you.*

ACT ONE SCENE TWO

THREE MONTHS LATER AND IT IS NOW SPRING.

As before, a bridge game in progress, except this time it is HUGH playing the hand out, watched by ISOBEL as dummy. There is complete silence as HUGH plays. JIMMY and VIC stare intently at their own hands, each in their own fashion.

ISOBEL gets up from her chair and stretches. She walks to the window and looks out. Finally, after an interminable wait, HUGH plays a card. JIMMY eyes VIC. ISOBEL wanders round the table to see what HUGH is about to play. JIMMY at once puts his cards face down and VIC holds her tightly to her chest. ISOBEL sees what HUGH is about to play but shows and says nothing, other than a slight raising of the eyebrows. HUGH concentrates on his hand. ISOBEL goes back to her side of the table and takes a large draft from the wine glass by her place. She sits still with her glass in hand and takes another draft. HUGH frowns at the card he was about to play then changes it for another in his hand. JIMMY glances at VIC who poker faces him back as she plays. HUGH looks back at his hand. Then back at dummy. He frowns, closes his eyes, stares blindly upwards, then plays a 'risk' card from dummy.

JIMMY quickly plays, winning the trick. VIC makes a purring noise. JIMMY plays again and again he and VIC win. ISOBEL puckers her face up. HUGH is about to play in response to the new lead then changes his mind. Silence. He takes a new card from his hand, puts it face down on the table, closes his eyes and thinks. JIMMY drums the table with his fingers. HUGH replaces the chosen card in his hand and takes another out. Same procedure. All wait for the play. HUGH finally rejects his choice, returns the card and plays his first choice. JIMMY shuts his eyes slowly. HUGH stares at the table. VIC'S frown deepens. JIMMY starts some more finger drumming. HUGH glances at him. JIMMY slowly stops.

                    JIMMY
We're ready when you are, Mr de Mille.
                    VIC
Some other time, Jimmy.

VIC plays. HUGH regards dummy's hand, goes to play one, thinks better of it, regards dummy again, then plays a second choice. JIMMY eyes HUGH, then produces the winning card from his hand and wins the trick. VIC collects the four cards JIMMY pushes at her across the table and taps them neatly into a trick. JIMMY is already playing his card for the next trick. Seeing it, HUGH glances at JIMMY who smiles sweetly back at him. HUGH ponders, then plays. VIC plays her card and seeing there is nothing he can do, HUGH plays a loser from dummy. VIC picks up the winning trick, taps them neatly into perfection and adds the second trick to her pile. VIC then plays, without expression. HUGH is momentarily transfixed when he realises he is in the middle of the cross fire then plays from dummy. ISOBEL slowly puts her hands on top of her head.

When HUGH has played from dummy JIMMY quickly produces another winning card for yet another trick. He pushes the four cards at VIC who does her collection routine, while JIMMY taps the fresh card he has just played with one indicative forefinger. HUGH plays what he knows is another losing card. VIC wins the trick and gathers. ISOBEL sticks her hands straight up into the air and pulls a face of slight unconcealed horror. HUGH'S face has gone rigid. VIC leads, and this time JIMMY produces a winner. ISOBEL puts her hands back down on to the top of her head and slowly closes her eyes. HUGH loses again. ISOBEL rises and pours herself another glass of wine then goes to stare out of the window.

HUGH plays and wins this trick and the next, accelerating as he thinks he has the rest of the tricks, only to be surprised by JIMMY produces one last surprise his hand - and picks up the winning trick.

      HUGH
We shouldn't have gone to game.

      ISOBEL
It was your call.

      HUGH
I shouldn't have gone to game.

      VIC
You went because I pushed you.

      HUGH
True.

      ISOBEL
Three spades would have given us game, Hugh. And the rubber. You weren't looking at the scorecard.

      HUGH
You're absolutely right. I let Vic push me.

JIMMY
Too late for tears. Water under the bridge. Whose deal?

ISOBEL
(going through the tricks)
You could have made it if you'd ruffed a club.

JIMMY
If ifs and ands were pots and pans there'd be no need for hypotheses.

VIC
That's one we haven't heard before.

JIMMY
I saw it on a motorway bridge. And you shouldn't scold your partner like that. There'll only be tears before bedtime.

ISOBEL
That's good coming from you. The number of times you've reduced poor Vic here to tears for over bidding or for not playing the hand the way you would have played it or whatever.

JIMMY
Talking of which - and here's something interesting - did you know that in her lifetime the average woman spends sixteen months in tears? Women cry for two hours and fourteen minutes every week.

VIC
I'm surprised it's not a great deal more.

ISOBEL
And I never knew there was such a thing as an average woman. Whose deal?

VIC
(to JIMMY)
How do you know how long women cry for anyway?

JIMMY
I read it in Gaga.

HUGH
Do you mean Saga?

JIMMY
The magazine for the increasingly invisible. You're not a subscriber?

HUGH
Not quite our age band. I meant it's certainly not Mary's.

JIMMY
You lucky dog.

ISOBEL
(with a sigh)
If you didn't feel like crying before, Vic, you might well feel like it now.

VIC
What I feel like doing most of the time would need censoring.

The door to the kitchen opens and MARY backs in carrying a laden tray. She is small, apparently shy and very pretty.

JIMMY
Let me do the door -
(getting up to help her)

MARY
I thought I heard voices.

JIMMY
Saints are always hearing voices.

VIC makes a sick face to ISOBEL and mimes sticking two fingers down her throat.

MARY
When I heard your voices I thought you'd probably like your sandwiches.

HUGH
Mary. You are a sweetheart.

JIMMY
And all this time you've been sitting out there in the kitchen?

MARY
No problem. I've got a book.

JIMMY
You could have read your book in here. Rather than out there in the kitchen.

MARY
It's no problem. Really.

VIC
Last time you were gracious enough to allow Mary to read while we were playing you had a small heart attack every time she turned a page.

JIMMY helps himself to a sandwich and ignores her.

VIC
(cont'd)
And as for when the poor girl was reading some comic novel and dared to titter -

JIMMY
Titter ye not - these are very good sandwiches, Mary. Very tasty indeedy.

HUGH
Mary makes really good sandwiches.

MARY
(moves on to ISOBEL)
Isobel? Sandwich?

ISOBEL
What's in them, Mary?

MARY
Parma ham. Mozzarella. And a very thin slice of green peppered chicken.

ISOBEL
Sounds irresistible. Ta muchly.

MARY
Take more than one. They're rather small.

ISOBEL
I shouldn't. I have to think of the old figure.

VIC
Less of the old.

JIMMY
So what's the book that's keeping you so quiet out there in the kitchen, Mary? Fifty Shades of something or other I'll bet.

MARY
No I'm reading Virgil's Aeneid actually.

JIMMY
(wrong-footed)
Right. Right.

ISOBEL
Virgil's Aeneid no less. Heavens. I haven't opened that since I was at school.

MARY
I've been meaning to read it for ages.

ISOBEL
How are you finding it?

MARY
Hard going as it happens. My Latin's awfully rusty. Another sandwich?

VIC, HUGH & JIMMY are distracted, reading something JIMMY is pointing out on a magazine. While their attention is taken, MARY stares at ISOBEL for a while before deciding to plunge in.

MARY
How are you? Are you okay?

ISOBEL
Yes. Yes I'm okay.

MARY
I haven't really seen you since the funeral.

ISOBEL
Well done. You said the F word. Well done.
        (silence)

MARY
Are you really all right?

ISOBEL
I'm better than I was. Much better than I was.
        (smiles briefly, and takes
         another sandwich)
These really are wonderful sandwiches.

MARY
Not everyone likes Parma ham.

ISOBEL
I do.

MARY
The really *good* Parma hams - they hang them up in the dark in these underground cellars.

ISOBEL
I don't know of any over-ground cellars.

MARY
Sorry?

ISOBEL
I was being facetious. I've developed a very bad habit of saying things facetiously.

MARY
I can understand that.
(regards her steadily/silence)
Some of the really old Parma hams they hang them up for years. Apparently that's what gives the ham its particular flavour.

ISOBEL
Life is just one long learning curve, isn't it.

ISOBEL wipes her mouth on a napkin that MARY provides.

ISOBEL (cont'd)
Thank you.

MARY
I'm really glad you're okay.

ISOBEL
That's really kind of you, Mary. Thank you.

MARY
I meant it.
(about to go)

ISOBEL
Would you have said anything if I'd said I wasn't okay?

MARY
I don't know. Probably not. Not a lot of us are any good at this, are we? Dealing with someone losing somebody.

ISOBEL
A neighbour - who's also a friend - the week after Tom died she crossed the street rather than have to speak to me.

MARY
I heard they're looking to treat grief as an illness now. With medication.

ISOBEL
Perhaps what grief needs to be treated with is education.

MARY
There's nothing anyone can say really, is there? I don't suppose.

ISOBEL
I don't suppose so either. Not really. But you know - all in good time. Time being the great healer.
(pause)

MARY
I have no idea of what you're going through. Sorry. I haven't the faintest what it's like. I haven't been there. The only loss I so called suffered was my mother dying. When I was two. Which I don't really remember at all.

ISOBEL
It's still dreadful. To have lost your mother that young.

MARY
I didn't know what it meant. I still don't really. As I said - she was the only person who I knew howver remotely who died. Which is probably why I'm not very good at this either.

ISOBEL
I don't agree. Most people just shy away. It's generally a case of sad looks and small noises. Most of all do not mention the name of the *departed*.

MARY
I'm sure. Anyway. Any time you feel like a chat.

ISOBEL
Thank you. You're really very kind. I've enjoyed talking to you.

MARY
Likewise.

MARY looks at her very directly, smiles then moves away, picking up discarded sandwich plates. ISOBEL watches her go.

VIC, wiping her mouth on one of MARY'S proffered paper napkins, detaches herself from the group and comes over to ISOBEL.

VIC
How's it going, pet?
(glancing at the busy MARY)
Been well counselled, have you?

ISOBEL
I've been talking with Mary. If that's what you mean.

VIC
That's one of Mary's things. Counselling. Only part time - but that's what she does. One of the many, many things she does.

ISOBEL
I get the impression you're not quite there in Mary's corner.

VIC
There's something a little spooky about Mary. Often the way with the quiet ones. You never quite know, do you. With the quiet ones.

ISOBEL
I think she's very genuine. I can see her counselling people. I'll bet she's rather good at it, because she's gentle but she listens. I'm sure that helps.

VIC
She doesn't do proper counselling. Like in bereavement counselling. No. No her line's more in victim counselling. Burglary victims. That sort of thing. Apparently.

ISOBEL
I always feel very sorry for people who've robbed.

VIC
I think they should chop the buggers' hands off.

ISOBEL
The victims'?

VIC
The burglars, you daftie. Breaking into people's homes and taking their belongings. I think it's a foul and rotten thing to do. Funnily enough before you arrived Mary was telling us of this poor bloke she had to go and counsel whose house had been broken into even though the thieves didn't take anything. Not a single thing. Apparently those are the cases that need the most counselling. When the burglars don't take anything.

JIMMY AND HUGH comes over with a magazine folded open. They are still laughing like schoolboys.

HUGH
We can't make out what this means.

JIMMY
(reading from magazine ad)
Caring, conservative, solvent -

VIC
You're not *still* on the dating page -

JIMMY
Caring, conservative, solvent -

HUGH
Probably means he likes sniffing glue.

VIC
(TO ISOBEL)
Little things, little minds.

JIMMY
You thought it were funny a minute ago.

HUGH
(taking the magazine)
Caring, conservative glue sniffer - N/S -

JIMMY
No sex.

VIC
Non smoker.

JIMMY
(taking magazine back)
You don't say. Non smoker, eh? Non smoker, right. Okay. o/c? Own - own cock -

VIC
Thank you, Jimmy.

JIMMY
Own cock -

VIC
Jimmy -

JIMMY
Own cocktail cabinet.
(grins at her)
But what suggestions do we have for GSOH?

ISOBEL
GSOH?

JIMMY
GSOH.

HUGH
Good sleeper own hair?

VIC
I somehow don't think so, Hugh.

JIMMY
Gets sexy on Horlicks. Has to be. So we have the ideal partner - a caring, conservative glue sniffer with his own cocktail cabinet, who does it all on Horlicks and would *WILTM?*

VIC
Would like to meet -

JIMMY
She knows, you know. Caring conservative solvent addict would like to meet affectionate lady of class and poise with an interest in car boot sales. One - I think - for the fair Isobella.
(hands her the magazine)

ISOBEL
Does anyone really answer these?

JIMMY
How else do you think I met Victoria Regina here?

HUGH
(takes magazine back)
We found one for Vic as well. Here we are: Heathcliff seeks his Cathy. Eighty two years young, wicked sod -

JIMMY
(taking magazine)
Come here.
(reads)
Wicked sod. Wicked *s.o.h.* Wicked sense of humour.

HUGH
You've got my glasses.

JIMMY
Eighty two years young, wicked sense of humour, o/z -

VIC
O/z?

JIMMY
Own Zimmer - wicked sod with own Zimmer seeks sensuous younger lady with whom to explore new boundaries. What are you waiting for, pet?

VIC
That's all we ever hear about these days - sex, sex, sex. I think it's got awfully stupid. If we're not all at it like monkeys in a tree then there's something wrong with us and we need to take something. It's just all so ridiculous, for God's sake. Asking our poor old bodies to do things they're way past doing. Like we were watching this film on the tele the other week with these two old fogies rekindling their childhood romance, and the next thing you know they're at it like a couple of badgers in a sack. Let's face it. Who are they kidding.

JIMMY
(to the tune of Hark the
Herald Angels)
Uncle Joe and Auntie Mabel -
Fainted at the breakfast table-
Take this as a solemn warning -
Never do it in the morning.

HUGH
(joining in)
Sanatogen has put 'em right -
Now they do it twice a night -

BOTH
Uncle Joe is hoping soon
To do it in the afternoon.

VIC
I don't know how I've stuck it, I really don't.

JIMMY
If you're not very careful, I'll tell on you. Now come on - back to the table.

They start to drift back to the table as MARY backs once more into the room carrying a tray with a LARGE BOWL on it and some smaller ones.

VIC
Oh. It appears our angel of mercy has brought us something more for our delectation.

MARY
It's nothing. It's just a dip. To keep you all going.

ISOBEL
May I?
(dipping a crisp in the bowl
and sampling the mix)
No that is *so* good. You made this? I must have the recipe.

MARY
It's pretty simple. You just take one jalapeno -

VIC
Ooh - and what's a *jalapeno* when it's at home?

MARY
A jalapeno's just a Mexican green chili pepper -

VIC
You mean a green chili? You could have said.
(sampling some)
It's a bit hot.

MARY
(to ISOBEL)
You chop the chilli, removing the seeds, crush a clove of garlic -

JIMMY
(sitting at table as VIC
tries the dip)
You eat any of that and it's the spare room for you tonight, Mrs Henshaw.

MARY
(continuing)
Add one cup of yoghurt - Greek - has to be Greek yoghurt - three avocados halved, pitted and scooped out, a level teaspoonful of red chili powder, juice of a lime and salt to taste.

HUGH
(sitting at table)
Makes the hair grow on your chest.

JIMMY
I'd rather something that makes it grow on your head.

ISOBEL
I'll never remember all that.

MARY
I can e-mail you the recipe. You're on line, I take it.

ISOBEL
Of course I am. Here.
(writes down address on a note)

MARY
(reads it)
Bellabella13@yahoo.com. Okay.

VIC
That's never your e-mail. Your e-mail's dinosaur50@yak-yak.

ISOBEL
That was my old one.

VIC
You might have said.

ISOBEL
I've only just changed it.

VIC
You still might have said.

JIMMY
You going to exercise the jaws all day? Or are we going to play some bridge?

ISOBEL
(to MARY)
Have you never tried to learn Bridge, Mary?

MARY
No fear. Friend of mine had to move not just house but county because of the way her husband behaved over the bridge table - and another couple I knew had just the worst divorce ever.

JIMMY
Marriage is grand, but divorce is fifty grand. Whose deal isn't it?

HUGH
I think it's Vic to deal.

ISOBEL
(to MARY)
I can't imagine that sort of situation between you and Hugh.

MARY
Maybe - but I'd rather not take the risk. Anyway. I have other interests.

ISOBEL
Your husband is a perfect gentleman to play with.

MARY
That's because he's not your husband. Like I said, Isobel - I don't want to run the risk. My friend who got divorced said she and her husband were forever going to bed arguing about what they should or shouldn't have bid. Or what they should have played and didn't. That's not for me. Like I said. I have other interests.
(looking ISOBEL in the eye)

JIMMY
Rabbit, rabbit, rabbit. It's like living on Watership Bloody Down.

MARY
(to ISOBEL)
Anyway. If I played bridge, you'd have no one to play with.

ISOBEL
I'm sure I'd find someone.

MARY
(still looking at her)
Yes. I'm sure you would.

ISOBEL
Something else to occupy me.

MARY
Better still.

JIMMY
Come on, Marjoram and Moneywort. There is still a rubber to be won or lost.

ISOBEL
(taking her seat but still talking to MARY)
I was trying the other day to remember how you two met. You and Hugh.

MARY
We met on something called a Trailblazer.

ISOBEL
A trailblazer? Sounds rather adventurous. Whose trail were you blazing?

HUGH
The Duke of Burgundy's.

ISOBEL
The Duke of Burgundy's no less.

MARY
And the Grizzled Skipper.

ISOBEL
Adventurous and romantic too. What fun.

HUGH
The Duke of Burgundy and the Grizzled Skipper are butterflies, Isobel.

ISOBEL
Butterflies?

MARY
Endangered British butterflies. It was a nature trail blaze.

ISOBEL
I didn't know you were an entomologist, Hugh.

MARY
He isn't.

HUGH
I'm not.

ISOBEL frowns at MARY, looks round at HUGH, then back to MARY.

HUGH
(cont'd)
It was after my divorce from Cathy had come through.

MARY
It's a very good way of meeting people.

ISOBEL
Butterflies?

MARY
Butterflies. Wild life. Ornithology. Cooking.

VIC
Bargello.

MARY
Sorry?

VIC
And has anyone seen my bloody glasses?

JIMMY
You could try looking on the top of your bloody head.

VIC
I can't try looking anywhere, clever clogs, till I find the bloody things.

She starts looking for her glasses.

MARY
(collecting dishes on to her tray)
It was this time of year, as a matter of fact. When we met. I just love this time of the year - when the light changes. And the evenings get longer. I always think things start to get better as it gets lighter.

ISOBEL
I used to get oddly depressed in Spring. When I was young. I always thought I'd fall in love in Spring. And I never did. I met Tom in the Autumn.

MARY
I love the autumn too. I love the smell of autumn.

ISOBEL
I suppose it's better than meeting in the winter.

MARY
Any time's good. If the time is right.

VIC
I've really got to stop doing this. I've got to stop losing my bloody glasses.
(staring blindly round the room)

ISOBEL takes VIC'S glasses from the top of her head and hands them to her.

VIC
(cont'd)
Oh. Ta.
(puts the glasses on and
frowns)
Except these aren't mine.
(staring accusingly at
ISOBEL)
You've got mine.

ISOBEL
I don't think so. Have I?

VIC
You daft brush.
(taking the glasses cff
ISOBEL)
These are my glasses.

ISOBEL
(trying the ones VIC has
given her)
These certainly aren't mine. Mine have got a bit of tape
holding them together here.
(indicating)

HUGH
(taking his off)
In that case I think I've got yours, Isobel.

VIC
Bloody things. They're a pain in the terminus. I suppose
now I need glasses to find my bloody glasses. Except I
can't afford 'em. Any idea what I paid last time for a
new pair of gregories?

ISOBEL
Gregories?

VIC
Gregory Pecks. Specs. Three hundred and sixty bloody
quid. For three hundred and sixty bloody quid I could
have a week in bloody New York.

HUGH
Or one night in a British hotel. Breakfast not included.

JIMMY
I thought we were meant to be playing bridge.

MARY
I'll leave the dip here.

                    ISOBEL
              (to MARY)
I'd like to hear more about these trailblazers sometime.

                    MARY
I'll e-mail you the name of the company that organizes
them.

                    ISOBEL
Thanks.

                    MARY
The company's called Pastures A-new. Not Pastures new.
Pastures *A*-new.

                    ISOBEL
Pastures A-new.

                    MARY
You never know. You never know what you might like till
you try it.

                    VIC
              (to ISOBEL)
Everyone's waiting on you, pet.

                    MARY
My fault. I've got to dash anyway. Friday night's my
tango lesson.

MARY picks up her tray of dirty dishes and goes.

                    ISOBEL
Tango lessons? That does sounds fun. Tango lessons.
              (sits at the table)
Interesting girl your Mary, Hugh.
              (picking up her hand)

                    HUGH
              (studying his
               hand/disinterested)
Absolutely.

                    JIMMY
Just a pity she doesn't play bridge.

                    VIC
I don't agree. No bid.

                    ISOBEL
Oh to be in England -
              (sorting her cards)
Now that April's there.

                              JIMMY
It's your bid, Longfellow.

                              ISOBEL
Browning actually. And everyone always misquotes him.
Everyone always says -
Oh, to be in England now that April's here -
When of course it's
Oh to be in England now that April's there.
                    (looking out after MARY)

                              JIMMY
Very interesting, teach - but it's still your bid.

                              ISOBEL
                    (still staring)
Because of course Browning was abroad at the time. When
he wrote it. Hence *now that April's there.*
                    (pause)

No. No bid.

                              JIMMY
                    (glances at her)
No bid.

SILENCE. HUGH clears his throat. Still no eye contact
with ISOBEL as she still looks out to where MARY is.

                              HUGH
Two clubs.

                              VIC
No bid.

They all now regard ISOBEL, who still dreams.

                              VIC
Your bid, Isadora.
          (silence)
Isadora? You to bid, petal.

ISOBEL still pays no heed.

                              JIMMY
Your bid, Duchess.
          (silence)

                              VIC
Your partner just bid two clubs.

ISOBEL
(long beat)
No bid.

STUNNED SILENCE.

VIC
Hugh's just opened two clubs, pet.

ISOBEL
So I heard.

VIC
The big two? As in you have to respond? You can't say no bid, pet. I mean you can - but you can't.

ISOBEL
And there was I thinking I just did.

HUGH
(generally)
Sorry about this everyone. I know I shouldn't. But -
(to ISOBEL)
Two clubs is a convention, Isobel. As I'm sure you know.

ISOBEL
A lot of things are conventions, as I'm sure you know, Hugh. Doesn't mean you have to follow them.

JIMMY
Sod the other conventions, love. This is bloody Bridge.

VIC
Jimmy's right. Two clubs is a forcing bid. You can't leave your partner in the lurch. You have to respond.

ISOBEL
I have responded. I said no bid.

VIC
How long you been playing this game, treasure?

ISOBEL
Way too long.

HUGH
You cannot leave me in two clubs, Isobel.

ISOBEL
Yes well I'm afraid I'm going to have to, Hugh. Sorry. No bid.

MARY comes through from the kitchen in her coat, ready to go.

MARY
Ciao, everybody. 'Bye.

VIC
Yes, we all know what ciao means thank you, love - Isobel pet -

ISOBEL
Excuse me.
(rising)
Mary? Hang on-

VIC
Now where do you think you're going?

ISOBEL
That all depends. Mary? Wait a minute, would you. Wait for me.

HUGH
Will someone please tell me what is going on? Isobel I have just opened *two clubs.*

ISOBEL
I'm perfectly well aware of the fact, Hugh. And knowing you, I'm also sure you'll make it.
(grabbing her coat and bag)
Mary - Mary I wonder if you'd mind taking me with you?

MARY
(stops)
That depends. Take you where?

ISOBEL
Wherever you're going. Anywhere. Perhaps I could come and watch you have your tango lesson.

MARY
If that's what you want. If that's what you'd like.

ISOBEL
Yes. It might be just the thing. Who knows? Come on.

MARY
Why not. Okay. Come on.

VIC
Hang about. Hang on - where do you think you're going?

                    ISOBEL
We're going dancing. Tangoing. It only takes two.

MARY and ISOBEL go. The OTHERS watch in stunned silence.
                    VIC
Well, well, well. Now what's up?
                    HUGH
Don't ask me. All I can say is I have twenty eight
points. Look.
          (displays his hand)
Twenty eight blooming points.
                    JIMMY
          (turning over ISOBEL'S hand)
And it would seem your partner had most of the rest.
                    VIC
So what was all that about then? What do you think's
going on now?
                    HUGH
I want to know what Isobel meant by saying no bid. No bid
- to a forcing two? Just look at this hand. Look. What
was Isobel doing?
                    JIMMY
Don't ask me, chum. God moves in such a mysterious way,
I'm convinced He's a woman.
                    HUGH
You don't get hands like this every day of the week.
                    VIC
Wonder what she was doing? Running off with Mary like
that?
                    JIMMY
Perhaps she buggered off because she don't want to play
no more.
                    VIC
Don't be ridiculous, Jimmy. I mean just suddenly upping
and running off. I don't get it. It just doesn't make
sense.
                    JIMMY
When did anything your *sex* do ever make sense?

HUGH
(looking at both his and his partner's hands)
This certainly just doesn't make any sense at all. We'd have had a grand slam in spades cold. It's a lay down in fact.
(showing them the two hands)

VIC
What I want is a reason for the all of a sudden exodus.

HUGH
Isobel must have taken leave of her senses. It's the only real explanation. She must have had a complete brainstorm. And if you'll excuse me for a moment, I need a tinkle.
(goes)

VIC
(calling after him)
First door on the left down the corridor. And don't forget to put the bloody seat back down!
(pause)
You want to hear what I think?

JIMMY
I'm going to anyway so why bother asking?

VIC
I think Mary has got the hots for Isobel.
(nods once)

JIMMY
The *what?* The *hots?* That's a bit Angela Brazil, isn't it? The *hots?*

VIC
You didn't see what was going on earlier. You were too busy giggling over the dating pages – so you didn't see what was going on over the sandwiches and the dip. All that stuff about holidays and things to do? Right? And then all the confidential chat to me about how gentle Mary is and how understanding and sympathetic – and then finally – and listen to this – there was stuff about not knowing whether you liked something or not until you had *tried* it. Yes? See where I'm coming from?

JIMMY
Even when it is bright and sunny without, your majesty, When I am with you I am enveloped in a nothing but very thick fog.

VIC
Okay, clever-clogs. So what do you think is going on? Let's hear your prize winning theory, shall we? That goes any way to explain as to why Isobel should get up from the bridge table and in the middle of a game which for once she was not losing - why she would abandon her partner who had just opened *The Big Two as in two clubs* - and go tangoing off into the sunset with weird and spooky *Mary.* Mary of all people?

JIMMY
My considered opinion is that poor Isobel still doesn't know what time of the day or the night it is and that maybe it seemed like a nice idea at the time.

VIC
That's just plain stupid. And boring. Mine's much more interesting. Infinitely more interesting. I like my theory. In our bosoms we could be nursing our very own Thelma and Louise.

JIMMY
Thelma and Louise weren't muff bumpers.

VIC
Weren't *what?*

JIMMY
Muff bumpers.

VIC
And what on earth is a muff bumper?

JIMMY
Muff bumpers are what you - my dear and lovely wife - believe Hugh's lovely wife Mary and our dear friend Isobel have suddenly and quite inexplicably become.

VIC
Where on earth did you get muff bumpers from?

JIMMY
Never you mind.

VIC
You know for a man of your age you Google far too much.

HUGH re-enters.

HUGH
So. So are we any nearer solving the riddle of the sands?

JIMMY
Vic here is convinced Mary and Isobel have eloped.

VIC
Jimmy -

HUGH
(laughing)
Eloped? How do you mean exactly? Eloped?

VIC
I was joking.

JIMMY
Hugh's not laughing.

HUGH
Only because I don't understand. What do you mean they've eloped? Mary and Isobel? Mary and Isobel?

JIMMY
Or possibly even Isobel and Mary.

HUGH
I don't understand what you mean by eloped.

JIMMY
She means they're off some place where they can push their beds together.

VIC
I meant nothing of the sort.
(eyeing JIMMY)
And I never said anything about them eloping. Why would I say such a daft thing.

JIMMY
Because you're in the habit of saying daft things?

VIC
If while you were out of the room I said anything unseemly or untoward, Hugh, it would only have been as a joke, I assure you.

HUGH
Of course. Of course it would.
(pause)
And I remembered to put the seat back down by the way.

VIC
Thank you, Hugh. Hear that, Jimmy? Hugh put the loo seat back down.
(JIMMY rises)
Now where you off to?

JIMMY
Where do you think. I'm going to ring the news room and tell them to hold the front page.

VIC
Very funny.

JIMMY
Not as funny as your theory about Isobel and Mary being carpet munchers.

HUGH
Carpet munchers?

VIC
Pay no attention. That's just Jimmy. *Trying* to be funny.

JIMMY
I know. Because nothing can quite match your comic notion of the Thelma and Louise eloping.

HUGH
Thelma and Louise? Weren't they - wasn't that that film?

VIC
All I was trying to say - while you were out of the room, Hugh - only to have Jimmy misquote me as always - was that nothing should surprise us nowadays. You know - such as for example - for the sake of argument say Mary and Isobel running off together. I mean every day you pick up the paper and sure enough someone somewhere or other has just come out of some closet or other somewhere, much to the general stupefaction of their nearest and dearest, so what I was trying to say was you know - anything goes. Only very recently there was that case of the two TV weather girls running off together - mind you, good riddance I say - then there was that big butch rugger player who kept saying he'd really have much preferred to have done ballet, and only last night on the television there was some shadow under-secretary of something or other on some chat show announcing to the world in general that he liked wearing lingerie at the State Opening of Parliament.

                    HUGH
Oh. Oh I see. I see where you're coming from. Yes. Yes
but even so. Even so the idea of Isobel and Mary being -
what was it?

                    VIC
                (hurriedly)
It doesn't matter. We know what you mean.

                    HUGH
I mean the very idea of it is ridiculous. Hilarious. Mary
and Isobel?

                    VIC
Right. So really it's none of our business why they did
go off together. So sudden like. On the spur of the
moment.

HUGH stops and looks thoughtfully at VIC. JIMMY frowns at
her.

                    JIMMY
I think that's quite enough on that subject, Blossom.
Don't you?

                    HUGH
Well we know Mary's reason. Mary was off to dance class.
I think.

                    VIC
And Isobel?

                    JIMMY
Isobel was just off her head. According to you.

                    HUGH
I didn't mean that literally. Although given what she's
just been through, it wouldn't be fair to expect her to
act altogether logically.

                    JIMMY
Right. It's just a crying shame it had to be when you
were holding the hand of the century. There won't be
another one like that for a while.

                    HUGH
I'm afraid you're right, Jimmy. There won't. When you
pick up a hand like that - with twenty eight points -

                    JIMMY
It's better than sex, eh? Even better than sex.

                              VIC
I'm surprised you can remember. Anyhow. Anyhow just for a
lark suppose it were actually true. And that Isobel and
Mary have bunked off together. Imagine. What would we do?

                              JIMMY
The first thing we'd do is to set about finding Hugh here
a new playing partner.

                              VIC
You are awful, Jimmy Henshaw. Worse than awful. You are
mega awful.

                              HUGH
But of course it's true, though. You would have to find
me a new partner.

                              JIMMY
We certainly would. However - however as far as this
evening goes, all is not lost, eh petal? In order not to
waste the evening entirely, how about a few hands of cut
throat?

                              VIC
Oh all right. Why not? I don't see why not.

                              HUGH
Cut-throat? You mean three handed bridge?

                              JIMMY
That's the idea. Three hands, we all bid for dummy.
                    (holding up a deck of cards)
There's no point in us just sitting here like wax works.

                              HUGH
What a good idea. Cut for deal?

As they all settle back sat the table.

                              JIMMY
Cut for deal -
                    (they cut)

                              JIMMY
And it's Mavis here to deal.

The cards are handed to VIC starts to deal.

                              HUGH
Mary and Isobel, can you imagine. What an idea.

                    VIC
I know. Funny, isn't it?

                   JIMMY
Hilarious.

                    HUGH
Isobel and Mary. I mean can you imagine.

The deal finishes and they pick up their cards and start
the ritual of sorting them. As they do behind them
through the uncurtained French doors the light in the
gardens is seen to change from pale early evening to a
most unseasonable warm red glow. Music is also heard, the
beat of the South American tango - and finally TWO
FIGURES appear, two women, MARY and ISOBEL slowly dancing
a South American tango - sensuous leg movements and all.
The card players are oblivious, because this is of course
just a picture in their respective heads..... apparently.
As the TWO WOMEN continue their slow dance, the BRIDGE
CARD PLAYERS continue to sort their cards.

MUSIC. Dave Brubeck. *Thank You.*

                  CURTAIN

ACT TWO SCENE ONE

One year later. Summer. The french doors are open and the early evening sunlight streams in.

At the card table sit VIC, JIMMY, HUGH and MARY. Things have changed. VIC plays with JIMMY as always, while now HUGH plays with MARY, who really isn't at all at home at the card table. Now it's Mary who is trying to play the hand at the start of the scene, watched by an increasingly nervous HUGH.

MARY
(stuck)
Help?

HUGH
You've got your crib.

VIC
She can't use her crib, Hugh. Not during play.

HUGH
She is still only *learning*, Vic.

VIC
She has been only learning, treasure, for some months now.

JIMMY
Months? Is that all it is? I feels like years.

HUGH
Jimmy Mary has only played what? Half a dozen times? Come on - be fair.

JIMMY
Be fair? We're not playing fair. We're playing bridge.
(noting what MARY is about to play)
Excuse me? Having no clubs?

MARY
What?

JIMMY
You're about to trump our trick so I was just making sure -that you have no clubs.

HUGH puts his hands on the top of his head.

MARY
I thought that was the point of trumps. For winning tricks.

JIMMY
Only if you have no more cards in the suit that's being played.

MARY
Why?

JIMMY
(slowly)
Because that is the rule.

VIC
Why?

JIMMY
Don't ask me - phone a friend.

MARY
(shrugs)
All right. But I don't see why.
(puts the card back in her hand and plays another)
I mean why have trumps at all? If you can't use them.

MARY plays and loses the trick. HUGH closes his eyes.

HUGH
They bid hearts, Mary. Remember?

MARY
If I'd remembered I'd have probably done something different.

HUGH
What exactly?

MARY
I don't know. But something different.

They play. MARY puts down a card with a certain amount of visible pleasure.

JIMMY
Having no spades.

MARY
Here we go again.

JIMMY
You're trumping my spade which is fine - if you don't have any spades.

MARY
Mind your own business what I have.

JIMMY
But you do have some spades.

MARY
Do I? And how do you know?

JIMMY
Because I can see your hand.

JIMMY pushes MARY'S hand which is just about visible to all back up to the accepted concealed position.

MARY
You shouldn't look at people's hands.

VIC
One peek is worth two finesses.

JIMMY
As Tom said to Lady Godiva.

MARY
Now I don't know what to play. Now I've completely lost the plot.

HUGH
Selling matches, sweetheart. You're selling matches.

MARY
(completely baffled)
What on earth are you babbling on about now?

HUGH
(slowly as if to a child)
There are people selling matches on London Bridge because they forgot to?

MARY
I don't know. Sign on?

HUGH
(looking at her again)
Because they forgot to -
(raises his eyebrows)

MARY
Because they didn't try harder at school? How should I know why there are these people selling matches on London Bridge, Hugh?

HUGH
They are selling matches because they forgot to *draw trumps*.

VIC
Have you never wondered why dummy is called dummy, pet?

MARY
But I've just been told not to play trumps if I have these other cards in my hand!

HUGH
No - no one told you that, sweetheart.

MARY
Oh yes they did. Not once - but twice. Not once but *twice*.

VIC
(with a sigh)
Come back, Isobel. All is forgiven.

JIMMY
That's nice.

HUGH
Actually that's not at all nice.

MARY
I am trying my best!

HUGH
She's trying her very best.

VIC
You know perfectly well what I mean. If Mary hadn't gone trogging off with Isobel that evening -

MARY
I did not go trogging off anywhere with Isobel. If anything Isobel went trogging off as you call it - with me.

JIMMY
What exactly does trogging entail? Sounds like a cross between trolling and snogging.

                        VIC
If you two hadn't gone running off together we'd still
have a status quo. Things would have been as they were.
Instead of like this. All ends up.

                        HUGH
Hang on. Hang on - wasn't it rather up to Isobel? What
she did or didn't do?

                        VIC
Hugh pet - for goodness sake. Just look what's happened.
Just look.

                        HUGH
I'm looking - and what I'm seeing is Isobel going off and
meeting someone and maybe - who knows? Maybe beginning to
come to some sort of terms with what's happened to her.

                        VIC
Hugh, pet. This someone Isobel she has met is fifteen
years younger than her.

                        HUGH
So? So?

                        VIC
Fifteen years?

                        JIMMY
Any chance of us finishing this hand? No I don't suppose
so there's a bat's really.

                        VIC
If you want my opinion I think everyone has taken leave
of their senses. Here we were, trying to get Isobel -
trying to get this friend of ours, this very *dear* friend
of ours - here we all were trying to help her through her
grief and her woe - and the next minute what's happening?
That self-same friend not only has upped and gone off
with her toy boy but that as far as you're all concerned
not only is it all right - it is far *more* than all right.

                        HUGH
No one is saying that exactly, Vic.

                        VIC
I don't remember hearing anyone saying anything exactly
contrary.

                        MARY
Please can we start this hand again? I haven't the
foggiest idea clue where I am or what I've played or what
I'm even meant to be doing.

JIMMY
There was a very vague hope once upon a moonbeam that you were meant to be playing bridge, treasure.

VIC
(sighing deeply)
If we're talking about what you thought you were doing, Mary pet, let's talk about what you were meant to be doing with Isobel, shall we? I mean that night. I mean just letting Isobel tag along like that.

MARY
I didn't 'let' Isobel 'tag along'.

JIMMY
I thought she were meant to be trolling - not tagging.

VIC
Didn't you think for one moment? Couldn't you see how *impressionable* she was? How vulnerable? Obviously not - obviously not otherwise you wouldn't have gone waltzing off to some salsa class or other.

MARY
It wasn't salsa. I don't do salsa. It was a tango class if you remember.

VIC
Oh and that's better, is it? That is altogether better?

MARY
Yes. Salsa isn't a proper dance.

VIC
And you think the tango is? Really? Then you can't have seen what they do on that programme. Their legs go everywhere. And you think that's a proper dance. All I can say is small wonder poor Isobel got all steamed up and threw all caution to the wind.

MARY
Where did you get all that from? Nothing like that happened at all. Isobel didn't throw anything to the wind, let alone her caution. She was sat there watching the class, then one of the instructors showed her a few steps - which she managed very well - then we went and had a glass of chardonnay across the road and then I drove her home.

VIC
And what happened when you had driven her home?

MARY
(perplexed)
What happened what?

VIC
Not all horses that are led to water don't drink, you know.

JIMMY
(rising)
I think we can kiss this hand good-night, one and all. So who's for a beverage? I know I most certainly am.

HUGH
Won't say no, James. Can't say I don't feel like one.

JIMMY
Can't say I don't feel like several.

The two MEN rise and go to the drinks table.

MARY
I really don't know what you're trying to insinuate, Victoria.

VIC
I am not insinuating anything, young lady. What I am saying is that we are leaving one rather vital element out of this story, don't you? Such as where Mr Incredible Hulk enters the frame.

MARY
It didn't happen the way you're trying to make out.

VIC
That were the night all this nonsense began.

MARY
It didn't begin at the tango class. The tango class had nothing to do with it.

VIC
If you hadn't seduced her into going with you that night none of this would ever have happened. Just think about it. If Isobel had stayed here playing bridge and not been spirited away to watch you doing the tango what has happened most definitely would *not* have happened.

JIMMY
Why are you trying to put this all on to poor Mary's shoulders?

VIC
Poor Mary indeed. If it weren't for poor Mary here we'd still have our bridge four.

JIMMY
What Isobel did she did of her own volition.

VIC
Yes. And the Pope is married with eight children. The night Isobel went off with poor little Mary here was the night she met the Incredible Hulk.

MARY
I wasn't at all the way you're suggesting. What actually happened was that just as we were leaving the class, Isobel saw this van in the car park that did fitted kitchens.

JIMMY
I'd like a van that could do that.

MARY
The people who give the dancing classes were having some work done in the house - and Isobel went back to have a look because she said she wanted to get her kitchen done and got this guy's number.

HUGH
Fair enough. You can't argue with that.

VIC
All I'm saying is that if your wife hadn't taken her off tangoing -

HUGH
Look at it another way, Vic. Maybe it's for the best. Maybe what's happened to Isobel is actually for the best.

VIC
What's the matter with you all anyway? This bloke is fifteen years younger than her! How can it possibly *do her good?* It's all wrong, you mark my words. And it'll all go wrong and all, that too.

JIMMY
Calm down and have a drink, love, and stop fretting yourself. You don't want to be up all night again walking the corridor with acid reflux.

VIC
And Jimmy you haven't put my roses in water!

JIMMY
Because I couldn't find the silver rose vase.

VIC
It was in the dining room. On the sideboard. Where it always is.

JIMMY
Well it's not there now, precious.

VIC
I put it there meself. You sure it's not there?

JIMMY
Positive.

VIC
(thoughtfully)
Oh. Right.

JIMMY
Victoria -

VIC
Later, Jimmy. Not now.

JIMMY
Not the silver rose vase. My mum gave us that.

VIC
Just put them in anything for the moment. Here -

VIC takes the roses and stuffs them into a water vase on the drinks table.

JIMMY
If I'm right in thinking what I'm thinking, petal -

VIC
Well you're not, Jimmy - okay?

JIMMY
I just don't bloody believe it.

VIC
I said later. Now then. Now where was I?

MARY
You were busy blaming all of us for what's happened to Isobel.

VIC
Yes. Yes well you do have to admit it's all changed since that evening. It was all going very nicely - and then that had to happen.

HUGH
From the way Isobel was behaving, my guess is that something was going to happen sooner or later.

VIC
Later would have suited me much better than sooner, thank you. Now I'm not blaming Mary. Mary can't help being pants at bridge. That's by the by. But what she could have helped was -

MARY
You are blaming me then!

VIC
I'm just saying, that's all. I'm just saying if you hadn't gone talking all alternative about tango classes and what spring did to your mojo and how to make these fantastic sandwiches you might still be out there dancing till dawn and we might still all be sat around here playing bridge as happy as clams in chowder.

HUGH
I don't know. Isobel sounded all right when I heard from her.

VIC
You heard from her? You never said.

HUGH
I had a card from her. Didn't you? From Goa. Said she was having a wonderful time.

VIC
From *where*? You never said.

HUGH
From Goa.

VIC
Goa? Well there you are then. Goa indeed. Need I say more?

JIMMY
It might be of interest. I didn't know that Goa was another of your special subjects.

VIC
I can tell you those places are nothing but trouble. Full of dope-heads, backpackers and - *Australians*. What can she have been thinking.

HUGH
Fun, maybe. Fun. Maybe she was thinking it might be fun.

VIC
At this age? Fun? Come on. We've reached the age now when they ask us how we want our beef - if we say well done they want to be paid in advance.

JIMMY
I like being my age. So far I've never been as old as this.

HUGH
I think possibly you may be jealous of Isobel, Vic.

VIC
Me jealous? What of? Don't be daft. What should I be jealous of? Other than the fact she's lost her husband.

JIMMY
Very funny ha-ha.

HUGH
It's in us all to want to kick over the traces.

MARY
Oh. Thank you, Hugh.

HUGH
I didn't mean that personally.

MARY
So how was I meant to take it?

HUGH
En passant. You were meant to take it en passant.

MARY
I might. If I knew what it meant.

The DOORBELL suddenly rings. They all REACT.

VIC
Now who on earth can that be?

JIMMY
There's a recognised way of finding out.

VIC
I hope it's not that awful man selling solar panels again.
       (going)

HUGH
Don't you just love it. Solar panels in our climate. Rain power's what we need.

JIMMY
Never. Wind's the answer to the nation's needs. There's enough of that in parliament alone to solve the energy crisis.

MARY
       (at the window)
You're not going to believe this.

JIMMY
It's obviously not the awful man selling solar panels then.

MARY
Quite very opposite.

VIC
       (reappearing)
Speaking of the devil - guess who the wind's blown in?

And enter ISOBEL, changed - not absurdly so but visibly changed. Tanned, slimmer, hair done differently, the style topped with a small sparkling butterfly, and she wears a few ethnic wrist bracelets, a carved necklace and some new silver finger and thumb rings. She is also apparently more confident.

ISOBEL
I know. I'm sorry but I did try ringing.

VIC
Did you? When?

ISOBEL
I got the machine. I left a message.

JIMMY
       (to VIC)
You and that machine. You never bloody check.

VIC
Am I the only one?

ISOBEL
I know - I know it's awful just to drop in without warning, particularly tonight of all nights - still bridge night I see by the by - but since we were passing right by your front door I thought perhaps you wouldn't mind.

JIMMY
Don't be daft. We're delighted to see you, sweetheart.

HUGH
We certainly are. How are you, Isobel?

ISOBEL
I'm good actually, Hugh. I'm good.

VIC
Oh - good no less. That's good. You being good.

ISOBEL
And you, Hugh? How are you?

VIC
And that's never easy to say. How are you, Hugh.

HUGH
I'm fine. Fine, Isobel. It really is lovely to see you.

He kisses her, a little too fondly perhaps, certainly a little too fondly for the watching MARY.

ISOBEL
Mary, dear.
         (taking both her hands)
Dear Mary.

MARY
Hiya.

ISOBEL
         (nodding)
Hiya.
         (embraces her)

JIMMY
Don't forget the diver.

ISOBEL
Would I ever?
         (embraces JIMMY)
And last but not least - Victoria. How are you, pet?

VIC
Me? I'm good too.

ISOBEL
Good. That is excellent. So okay. Big hug.
(gives her a big hug)

JIMMY
And you couldn't have timed your return to the fold better. We're all just about to paint our noses red.
(holding up bottle)

ISOBEL
No - no not for me, Jimmy. I've given up alcohol.

VIC
You what? You never.

ISOBEL
I certainly have. And lost the best part of a stone.

VIC
I'm not sure it suits you.

ISOBEL
(laughs)
You you wouldn't be. That wouldn't be you, would it. That wouldn't be our Vic. Now before I forget - which is one of the reasons for my visit - I've bought you all something.

She starts looking in her large carrier bag.

HUGH
I think it suits you, Isobel. Losing weight. I think you look - wonderful.

MARY eyes him.

VIC
(to ISOBEL)
You did say 'we' were passing by your door, didn't you? So where is he? The other half of the 'we' bit?

ISOBEL
Alan? He's had to go and see a client. A prospective client.

VIC
At this time of day?

ISOBEL
The curse of the self-employed. Here we are.

ISOBEL produces some wrapped gifts.

JIMMY
It's not a bit like Christmas.

VIC
You say that every year.

ISOBEL
For the girls - and for the boys.

She hands VIC and MARY their presents and HUGH and JIMMY theirs. VIC takes out of her bag a long patently transparent brightly hand dyed sari and regards it as MARY does the same.

VIC
Oh. My.

MARY
This is lovely, Isobel. Thank you.

VIC
Yes. Ta. Just the thing for wearing round Morrisons.

ISOBEL
(laughing)
Strictly home wear only. For chilling out.

VIC
I see. Well we do a lot of that these days. What with the cost of the central heating.

MARY
I think they're cool, Isobel. Really cool.

JIMMY
They certainly are, petal. In fact if you're intending to chill out in those, you'd better get out your thermals.

HUGH has opened his present and stands regarding a small wooden carving.

HUGH
This looks intriguing. What is it exactly, Isobel?

ISOBEL
It's a Goanese love charm.

HUGH
(nodding)
A Goanese Love charm?

JIMMY
That what this is as well?
(holding up his own small
wood carving)

ISOBEL
And I have to tell you they work.

JIMMY
They do? How? I do hope they don't involve insertion.

VIC
(trying not to laugh)
Jimmy -

ISOBEL
(seriously)
They're empowered.

JIMMY
You don't say. Batteries included?

ISOBEL
No seriously, Jimmy. They come from this indigenous tribe that's renowned for their sexual prowess. They really do work.

JIMMY
Maybe. But I think I'll stick to single malt.

VIC
So. So how was Goa, pet? I hope you remembered your Diocalm.

ISOBEL
We were only in Goa for a few days, Vic. We spent most of our time in Rajkadistan. You have no idea what that country is like. It is so vibrant. The people. And the colour.

VIC
And the khazis.

JIMMY
You know our Vic. She won't go anywhere where the geography doesn't work.
(handing round drinks)
The Queen may travel with her personal loo seat, but if madam here had her way she'd travel with her own *en suite*.

ISOBEL
You don't know what you're missing, people. There's this whole other world out there.

VIC
I'm sure. And if ever I want to experience it I can always take a day trip down the Edgware Road. So now. Sit you down and tell us all about Mr Wonderful.

ISOBEL
Of course. Of course you haven't met him yet, have you?

VIC
Mary here has.

ISOBEL
I don't remember Mary meeting him.

VIC
The night of the great fandango.

MARY
I didn't. I saw him very briefly. Talking to Isobel in the kitchen.

ISOBEL
I didn't think you'd met him. Don't worry - you're all going to meet him - in due course. He's quite a remarkable guy.

JIMMY
Does he play bridge?

ISOBEL
As a matter of fact that is one of the few things he does not do, Jimmy.

VIC
Fancy that. So what's the big thing you have in common then?

ISOBEL
All manner of things. As I said, he's a very interesting guy. Into all sorts of things. Speaks three languages, he plays the guitar, he can cook - and he listens.

MARY
And he fits kitchens.

ISOBEL
He *makes* kitchens, Mary. He designs them. And builds them.

VIC
And he listens.

ISOBEL
Yes. Yes. He does. He's a very *good* listener. Look - it's all right - I know what you're thinking.

VIC
We're not thinking anything, pet.

ISOBEL
Course you are. You're thinking what on earth does Isobel think she's doing with some guy ten years younger than her.

VIC
Ten years? He's ten years younger than you, is he, pet?

ISOBEL
I'd be just the same in your shoes. It's only natural. But when you meet him you'll understand.

VIC
It's none of our affair, pet. It's not our business - what you do or you don't. Now tell us more about Africa.

ISOBEL
India.

VIC
India then. What inspired you to go there in the first place. Let's hear all about it.
            (patting the sofa beside
             her)

ISOBEL
I wouldn't mind a soft drink if you have one, Jimmy. Do you have any elderflower?

JIMMY
No but we've a ton of bindweed. I can offer you a tonic water.

ISOBEL
Tonic water would be lovely. With a dash of angostura if you have it. And a slice of lemon. And some ice.

JIMMY
Sure you just wouldn't prefer a bloody great vodka?

ISOBEL
Really - I can't tell you how much better I am not drinking. I sleep for a start. And I have so much more energy.

VIC
Which is what you need, pet. Knocking around with some fellah who's fifteen years younger than you.

ISOBEL
Ten actually.

VIC
Ten. Right. If you say so.

ISOBEL
What is this great thing about age? I do wonder. The way we go on about it. As if age difference is some sort of crime. I'd have thought compatibility was more important. I can't see why it should matter so dreadfully if a man is a few years younger than a woman if what they have is true compatibility.

VIC
Look at it another way, pet. It is a fact that when women are born we're born quite a lot older than men. When boys and girls are one year old we are actually at least five years old so that when we're sixteen boys are still practically sucking their thumbs. Even though according to their birth certificates they're the same age as us. So by that token your boyfriend Adam -

ISOBEL
Alan. His name is actually Alan.

VIC
Right. So by that very token your boyfriend Alan who you say is ten years younger than you is actually more like twenty years younger if not more, so that when you're ninety he'll be only in his fifties. And probably taking a good look around him.

ISOBEL
You can say and think what you will, Vic, but in the end that is Alan's concern really.

VIC
And what about your concern? Don't Alan's concerns concern you?

ISOBEL
I'm afraid that's my business. They might do and there again they might not.

VIC
I take it he's not moving his stuff in then.

ISOBEL
What's it to you whether Alan moves his stuff in as you put it or not? That's really none of your business.

JIMMY
Girls. Girls -

VIC
Yes - well it is some of my business, pet. I'm your friend. We go back a long way. And as far as I'm concerned what happens to you -

ISOBEL
Nothing is going to happen to me.

VIC
All I'm trying to say is that I'm here for you. I am right behind you.

JIMMY
And behind every woman stands a man wondering what he said wrong.

HUGH
I like that, Jimmy. That's very funny, Jimmy.

VIC
Don't worry. It's not original.

ISOBEL
What is? Alan often questions what is actually original. He says everything is organic. That light and sound come from the same sources - and emotions spring from the same wells. We may change the steps but what we are doing is still dancing. Everything is already in place and always has been.

VIC
(staring at Isobel)
You don't say.

ISOBEL
That's what Alan says.

VIC
He's obviously got a way with words, your Alan.

ISOBEL
I told you. He's a very interesting man. And because Alan listens, I can talk to him. I can tell Alan things, discuss things with Alan - in a totally different way than I can with anyone else.

VIC
Well of course. Just so. Naturally. Of course you can tell him things you can't tell us. He doesn't know a thing about you.

MARY
Oddly enough I find the same thing with counselling. It's much easier to counsel someone you know nothing about than someone you do.

ISOBEL
Alan doesn't counsel me, Mary love. Alan and I talk. We relate.

VIC
Yes I'm sure, pet. But what I'm saying is don't you think it's a little soon? You know. To be relating with someone brand new.

ISOBEL
No I don't as it happens. I don't think so at all.

VIC
Fine. On your head be it then. But if you ask me which you won't - I'd say you were asking for trouble.

JIMMY
And I'd say you've said quite enough, Petal.

VIC
I'm only trying to help, Jimmy.

JIMMY
Which is always when you're at your most dangerous.

ISOBEL
It's all right, Jimmy - I can handle myself. Thanks to Alan I've found out not just how to be but what to be.

VIC
You must let me have the recipe, duck.

ISOBEL
Don't mock, Victoria. Alan's taught me how to stand up. How not to be in denial. How to recognise what is happening and how to relate. How to stop growing invisible. How to stop apologising for existing. Alan talks very differently. He says things in a very different way. In ways very different from the ways I used to use - and which some of us still do.

VIC
He is a whole lot younger, pet. I mean twenty years.

ISOBEL
Ten years actually.

VIC
Let's split the difference and settle for fifteen, shall we?

ISOBEL
Alan is only interested in truth, Vic. According to Alan the key to life lies in speaking the truth.

VIC
Oh come on. Can you imagine? If we all went round speaking the truth there'd be absolutely nothing to talk about.

ISOBEL
Fine. Take that for an example. What you just said. That is a form of the truth because it's what you *feel,* Vic. That is what we have to get from life. What we truly feel and what we truly want.

HUGH
No I go for that. I think what Isobel's saying is possibly right. That the truth is the most important thing. Your own truth. The truth that's actually inside us.

MARY
You don't really believe that, Hugh.

HUGH
Does that surprise you?

MARY
So everything you say is the truth.

HUGH
I wouldn't go as far as to say everything. But I try not to lie. I do try.

MARY
There are all sorts of things you say that aren't true.

HUGH
I try very hard not to lie.

MARY
And sometimes - equally - you try very hard not to tell the truth.

VIC
(to ISOBEL)
Your Mr Wonderful certainly has quite a knock on effect.

ISOBEL
Look - look I can't speak for all of you. I can only speak personally. And for me - Alan has helped me more than I can say.

VIC
And didn't we? Didn't we help you? We tried our best, you know.

ISOBEL
Of course you did. You were wonderful.

VIC
I'm sure we weren't. But we did try.

ISOBEL
It's often much harder for friends.

VIC
So Alan did more. Alan did more for you.

ISOBEL
No. No he just did things that - that were different, that's all. He just came at things from a different angle. This isn't a competition, Vic dear - really it isn't.

ISOBEL smiles at VIC and embraces her.

VIC
Okay.

ISOBEL
Okay.
(changing the subject)
I see The Lady in the Hat is still missing.

JIMMY
Not the only thing.

VIC
The first chase was a bit of a wild goose one. She's now in the hands on another expert.

JIMMY
Yet another expert.

MARY
The Lady in the Hat being?

HUGH
This picture of Jimmy and Vic's.
(to MARY)
I don't understand what you meant -

ISOBEL
It's not a picture, Hugh. It's a painting. A painting Jimmy and Vic think might be by an Old Master.

MARY
Okay. I see. Like on that programme.

VIC
Like on that programme, pet. You got it.

MARY
Do you know a lot about art then, Victoria?

JIMMY
Know a lot about art? Our Victoria? Let me tell you Victoria knows all there is to know about art. She just doesn't know what she likes.

ISOBEL
(to MARY)
You don't remember the Lady in the Hat?

MARY
I tend not to really notice peoples' pictures.

VIC
Oh dear. Bang goes another infinitive.

MARY
Sorry?

VIC
Infinitives. Isobel's allergic to split infinitives.

MARY
(stares at VIC and ISOBEL blankly)
Oh. Right. What are they?

VIC
Don't ask. Unless you're awarding prizes.

JIMMY
Didn't you know it's rude to correct other people's grammar? What you're doing when you do that is telling the other person you're better h'educated than what they are.

VIC
So what? Isobel generally is.

MARY
If this painting - that isn't here -

JIMMY
And probably never again will be -

MARY
If it was by someone famous, and if it is worth a lot of money -

JIMMY
It won't be.

MARY
So why do you think it might be? I mean where did you get it?

VIC
We got it at a house clearance sale yonks ago, if you really must know.

JIMMY
And that's all we know about it, love.

VIC
Right. It didn't come with any providence.

HUGH
I think you may mean provenance.

JIMMY
Never. Provenance is that place in the south of France.

MARY
Even so, it could still be valuable. And suppose that it is?

JIMMY
No problem. If it's worth anything we won't ever see it again. As in the silver bon-bon dish. As in me mum's lovely rose vase.

VIC
(sighing)
Jimmy -

JIMMY
Sorry, petal. Just following Isobel's new mantra.

ISOBEL
Talking of which I really must be going. Alan's got to collect this Harley he's just bought from some bloke on e-bay and then we're going on to see The Boy with His Foot in his Mouth.

VIC
New friend of yours?

ISOBEL
You haven't seen him. You must. He's this new stand up everyone's raving about. He's on at The Convenience.
(to blank stares)
You haven't been there either, have you? I must take you both. Those amazing old public lavvies at South Cross Junction? They're now a brand new a comedy venue.

VIC
You don't say. Do you have to take your own seat?

JIMMY
No - but you have to be flush to afford it.

VIC
They should book you in there, Jimmy.

JIMMY
I shall get on to my agent at once.

ISOBEL
I really must go. Sorry.

VIC
So off you go. There's nowt spoiling.

ISOBEL
Nowt spoiling?

VIC
It's just an expression. Something my dad used to say.

ISOBEL
Nowt spoiling. I rather like that.

VIC
Don't let me catch you using it. Go on. You mustn't keep Adam waiting.

ISOBEL
Alan.

VIC
Or him either.

ISOBEL
Bye, all.

MARY
Isobel -

ISOBEL
Mary.

MARY
Can I ask you something quickly?

HUGH
It can wait, Mary.

MARY
No it can't, Hugh. Anyway, you agreed.

HUGH
Poor Isobel's in a hurry.

MARY
(to ISOBEL)
It's just a small favour.

ISOBEL
Of course. What can I do for you, Mary dear.

MARY
Hugh's just drawn all this money down from his pension fund -

HUGH
You don't have to go into details, Mary -

MARY
He wants to spend some of it on the house -

HUGH
We want to spend some of it on the house.

MARY
On a new kitchen actually - so what we were wondering -

HUGH
What you were wondering -

MARY
Was we were wondering if we could borrow Alan.

A brief silence.

ISOBEL
You want to borrow Alan?

HUGH
(laughs)
In a purely professional capacity.

MARY
That kitchen he built for the dance people -
(shakes her head)
Wow.

ISOBEL
He's really not mine to loan really. Why not just ring him yourself?

MARY
I don't think that would be right.

VIC
I should cocoa.

ISOBEL
I'm not Alan's keeper.

MARY
It really would be better coming from you.

ISOBEL
Mary dear. You just ring him yourself. I'll give you his mobile -

MARY
I don't know him.

ISOBEL
Most of his customers don't know him.

MARY
I know. But you do.

ISOBEL
I do what?

MARY
You know him. And you know us. So if you asked him -

VIC
They could jump the queue.

MARY
Please?

ISOBEL
There's no guarantee he'll say yes. He's very busy.

MARY
If he could just come round and give us an estimate -

HUGH
Don't push it, Mary.

ISOBEL
No it's all right, Hugh. It's perfectly all right. Okay. Okay I'll mention it to Alan.

MARY
Mentioning it isn't the same. I'd rather you asked him.

ISOBEL
(finally)
Okay.
(with a smile)
Okay I'll ask him.

MARY
Great. I'm like - I'm like *wow. Wow.*
(hugs ISOBEL)

ISOBEL
Wow. And I'm like - I'm like *wow.*

VIC
When what you should really be like is like why.

ISOBEL looks at her. VIC poker faces her back.

MARY
(hugging ISOBEL)
You are such a doll.

ISOBEL
(worried)
Thank you, dear. Right. Right I really must dash. Bye, one and all.
(blows kisses to them all in
 farewell)

VIC
(as she gets kissed)
Send my love to The Boy with His Finger in his Nose.

ISOBEL
The Boy with His Foot in His Mouth.

VIC
Might be best to reserve your judgement.

ISOBEL goes.

MARY
I am so excited. This is so cool.

HUGH
Don't start jumping about, Mary. Isobel asking him doesn't necessarily mean he'll say yes, you know.

MARY
He'll say yes, Hugh. When he finds out what I want I just know he'll say yes.

LIGHTS DOWN

MUSIC

ACT TWO SCENE TWO

Autumn.

The curtains are open but the light and the landscape without has changed from the clear bright light of summer to the gold of late autumn.

ISOBEL and VIC are religiously and ritualistically preparing the card table like attendants at the altar, getting the box of two packs of cards and setting out the pencils and the score pads, and anything else that is needed for the game.

VIC
I don't think I'm really up for this.

ISOBEL
We can't just go on like nothing's happened. It's been over three months.

VIC
We've observed all the niceties. Written to him. You rang him.

ISOBEL
And I always get the machine.

VIC
I really don't know what else we can do. And I still say we're being previous. Just like I said we were with you - And look what came of it.

ISOBEL
You could say good things came of it.

VIC
I don't see as how. You went gallivanting off to Africa -

ISOBEL
India. And what happened to your card table?

VIC
Never you mind. And it's only temporary.

ISOBEL
And where are your chairs?
(the chairs are now ordinary kitchen chairs)
I thought you were going to be firm.

VIC
You try being firm with Annie. It's like putting your foot out to stop a bus.

ISOBEL
She hasn't gone off with your lovely card table.

VIC
Only to have it valued. She's just taken it off to get it priced.

ISOBEL
You are far too trusting. Far too trusting.

VIC
Which of course you are not. Not at all.

ISOBEL
What I am or am not is beside the point. This point in particular. And what happened to your lovely little Persian rug?
(noticing the missing top rug)
Don't say.

VIC
Ssssh. Put a sock in it - he hasn't noticed it's gone yet.

As JIMMY ENTERS carrying some bottles that he places on his drinks table.

JIMMY
(mock tragic)
Once more unto the breach, dear friends. Once more.

VIC
Very funny I don't think.

JIMMY
Are you *sure* you're doing the right thing?

VIC
Are you sure *we're* doing the right thing. You live here as well, pet.

JIMMY
I think it's asking for trouble. Poor bugger's hardly had time to turn around.

VIC
It's been well over three months.

JIMMY
He still won't know what's hit him.

ISOBEL
I think three months is plenty enough time.

JIMMY
It wasn't enough time for you, pet.

VIC stands back and admires the setting on the card table.

JIMMY (cont'd)
You went gallivanting off to the West Indies -

VIC
To Africa.

ISOBEL
India.

JIMMY
Off you went with your hairy biker -

ISOBEL
If that's a reference to Alan -

VIC
Pay no attention, duck. As they say not all men are as awful. Some are dead.

ISOBEL
I'd rather we forgot all about me and concentrated instead on what has happened to poor Hugh.

VIC
Yes - and particularly the way it happened. Right out of the blue. Without as much as any warning. None of us saw that coming. Did you spot anything? See any signs? I certainly didn't.

ISOBEL
I did actually think that lately Mary had a rather odd look to her.

JIMMY
You and your looks.

VIC
Go on, Isadora, because I thought just the same. That night you dropped when you'd just come back from wherever? And you were off to see some daft comic or other -

ISOBEL
Who incidentally was *very* unfunny.

VIC
I did think there was something distinctly odd about Mary that evening.

JIMMY
I didn't. I thought she looked smashing.

VIC
There's new for you.

ISOBEL
We're not talking about her appearance, Jimmy. We're talking metaphysically.

JIMMY
Metaphysically. Oh. Right. Excuse me. I thought you were talking meteorologically.

ISOBEL
You can tell a lot from people's aura, Jimmy. From their ambience. Their look. For instance peoples' faces sometimes go very strange shapes.
            (to VIC)
I said as much to you once. Not so very long ago.

JIMMY
Vic's face has always been that funny shape. I'm going to get some ice.
            (goes)

VIC
You know Mary did have a very strange look to her that night. But even taking that into consideration we have to say it were very sudden.

ISOBEL
Interesting to hear if Hugh noticed anything untoward.

VIC
Do you think we can go there, pet? It still is a rather soon. I think this is a case of softly-softly, don't you?

ISOBEL
I don't know. There were times - personally speaking - there were times when I could have perhaps done with people being a little less general and a little more particular.

VIC
I thought by and large that's what we were. What we always are. Particular. Rather than general.

ISOBEL
Of course you are. Of course. That's the sort of people you both are. I was referring to other people. But as far as this evening goes perhaps it would best keeping a low profile - because if anything's to be said it might be better to let it come from Hugh.

VIC
I think that's probably best, you know. We can only do so much and no more. We can only do what friends should be doing for each other. Being there. Stepping up to the plate. That's all that matters.

ISOBEL
Let's just hope we're not found wanting.

JIMMY returns with ice tray and bucket.

JIMMY
I don't know about you two, but I could do with taking the edge off.

VIC
Yes. Good idea. Let's have a Queen.

ISOBEL
A Queen.

ISOBEL
Apparently before leaving the Palace Her Majesty likes to have a little nip.

JIMMY
And not from the corgis.
            (sings as he fixes drinks)
She has an itsy, bitsy, teeny, weeny, little royal dry martini -

VIC
You'll have one too, won't you love?

ISOBEL
I think I will. Under the circumstances.

JIMMY
That's the ticket. Got to keep going, petal. Got to keep going.

VIC
I bet you feel better coming off the wagon, don't you?

JIMMY
(fixing drinks)
Course she does. You can have enough of waking up in the morning knowing that's the best you're going to feel all day.

VIC
Here we go. Yet another chance to hear those you have loved.

JIMMY
I tell you when I read about the evils of drinking I gave up reading.
(still fixing the drinks)

VIC
It's like having your very own stand up parrot.
(takes a sip of her drink)
Not that I find any of them new comedians funny. I haven't found anyone funny since Tommy Cooper. Oh and Les Dawson. I loved Les Dawson. He did make me laugh.

JIMMY
(doing his LES)
You know when I was born - when I was born I was so ugly the midwife slapped my mother.

ISOBEL
(taking drink from JIMMY)
Thank you, Jimmy. And when Hugh finally gets here -

The DOORBELL suddenly rings and when it does VIC suddenly grabs ISOBEL'S hand.

VIC
And my God that's him and he's early.

ISOBEL
Are you sure it's him?

JIMMY
(looking out of a window)
It's either him or a top notch impersonator.

VIC
He would be early, wouldn't he.

ISOBEL
Better than being late, surely.

VIC
I prefer late. Being early's just plain rude. So go on then. Go and let him in.

ISOBEL
Excuse me. But isn't this your house?

VIC
It might be but he's your friend!

ISOBEL
It's your house.

VIC
You knew him first! Go on! *Go on!*

ISOBEL
Oh very well. Very well.
(goes)

VIC
Yes. Yes well you know what I think, don't you.

JIMMY
No I don't. And when I want your opinion I'll give it to you. And I'll tell you something else. You know what Mark Twain said about cauliflowers? He said they're nothing but cabbages with a college education.

VIC
I don't know what you're on about. Why do you go on like that?

JIMMY
Don't know. Just treading water I suppose.
(downs his drink))

As JIMMY puts his glass down and out of sight the door opens and ISOBEL re-enters.

ISOBEL
It's Hugh everybody.

JIMMY
All hands on deck.

HUGH enters.

VIC
Hugh. Hello, Hugh.
(embraces him)
It's very good to see Hugh, you. To see you, Hugh.

HUGH
It's good to see you too, Vic. Jimmy.

JIMMY
Salut, old thing. Salut.

VIC
Less of the old.

HUGH
Sorry if I'm a bit early.

VIC
Early? Not a bit of it. Anyway - anyway early's nice. Means we get to see more of you.

HUGH
Sorry - but I just had to get out of the house.

VIC
Course. It couldn't matter less. Really.

HUGH
I'm so used to always running late that now I find I'm always early.

VIC
I don't even know what the time is.

ISOBEL
It's only twenty to six.

VIC
Twenty to six. There you are.
(smiles)
Only twenty to six. It feels much later.

JIMMY
It certainly does. Feels more like ten to six.

VIC
Doesn't it? Doesn't it just? Probably something to do with getting older.

HUGH
Right. Right.

JIMMY
Right. Right so what about a drink, old chap. Let me fix you a special Jimmy special.

HUGH
Thank you but no thank, Jimmy. I'm not drinking. That was the first thing I did of course. Hit the bottle. So I'm off it. Been off it for quite a while. But don't let me stop you.

ISOBEL
You're not. Because we're not drinking either. As you can see.

HUGH
I followed your lead, Isobel. Coming off the drink.

VIC
Oh your friend Isobel's back on it.

ISOBEL
(with an attempt at a laugh)
No I'm hardly *back on it*, Vic. Just the occasional glass of wine. Socially. That's all.

HUGH
(pause)
I was drinking a couple of bottles of wine a day.

VIC
It's understandable.

ISOBEL
And it's easily done. It's very easily done. But you're right to come off it, Hugh. Last thing you want to do it on is booze. You stick at it until you're through this.

HUGH
I fully intend to.

JIMMY
Ah well - *chacun á son gout*, as I always say without knowing what in hell it means. *Chacun á son gout.* Although personally - personally I'd always rather have a bottle in front of me -

VIC
Old fans may remember this one.

JIMMY
I'd rather have a bottle in front of me than a prefrontal lobotomy.

HUGH
I trust there isn't any danger of that.

JIMMY
I hope so too. Not that I know what it is exactly.

ISOBEL
It's a perfectly dreadful medical procedure they used to do to people. Mental patients. And not always mental patients.

HUGH
I'm sure. Anyway - as long as there's no chance of it being done to Jimmy.

VIC
I don't know. Sometimes I think it mightn't be such a bad thing.

HUGH
Well anyway. What's been occurring? You been playing much bridge?

ISOBEL
Bridge? I don't think so. Have we, Vic? No I don't think we've really been playing hardly any bridge at all hardly.

VIC
Hardly at all. Been stuck for a fourth, you see.

HUGH
That's my fault. Sorry.

VIC
(hurriedly)
Of course it weren't your fault, pet. Don't be so stupid. I mean daft. Don't be so silly.

ISOBEL
If it was anybody's fault it was mine.

HUGH
I don't see how on earth it could have been your fault, Isobel. I don't see how that could have been possible. Right. So are we planning to play or aren't we?

ISOBEL
We don't have to play.

JIMMY
Course we don't. We can just sit round here not drinking instead.

HUGH
But I thought that was the whole idea of this evening.
To get together again and play.

ISOBEL
Only if you're all right, Hugh. Only if you're feeling up
to it.

HUGH
Up to it? I've been looking forward to this enormously.
To playing again.
        (beat)
To seeing you. To seeing you all, that is.

ISOBEL
Good. So how shall we play then? Same as before?

HUGH
Unless you want to change partners.

ISOBEL
Why should I want to change partners. Do you want to
change?

HUGH
Me? No. No only if you wanted to.

ISOBEL
I don't want to change. But you might - because you're
the one who's been stuck with me.

HUGH
I can't think of anyone I'd rather be stuck with. So if
everyone else is happy.

VIC
Absolutely. I'm sure the very last thing poor Hugh wants
is a new partner. Under the circumstances.
        (smiles, a smile which fades
        to frown as she realises)

JIMMY
So if we're all met - to table then. Okay?

HUGH
Fine.

They take their places at the table.

VIC
Good. Right. Cut for deal -
   (as they do and look what
    card they have cut)
And it's -

JIMMY
It's me to deal.

HUGH cuts the fresh pack to him and JIMMY deals. As he does HUGH suddenly smiles at ISOBEL.

VIC
That's nice. It's nice to see you with a smile on your face, Hugh.

JIMMY
Where else might he have it?

HUGH
You mean perhaps I shouldn't have a smile on my face. Yes?

VIC
Well no. Well yes and no. I do and I don't. I mean on the one hand it's not a particularly smiley *moment* -

HUGH
No?

VIC
Well - well no. No.

They look at him. Even JIMMY who stops dealing for a moment.

HUGH
You don't know. It might be.

VIC
You what? It might be? I don't quite cocoa.

ISOBEL
Maybe we should let Hugh speak, Vic. Perhaps we should hear what he has to say.

HUGH
Thank you, Isobel. And I know you'll understand because you've been through the mill as well. Although through something worse, I have to say. Infinitely worse.

ISOBEL
I don't necessarily agree, but still. Go on, Hugh. Go on.

HUGH
I know what you're all thinking, I really do - because if it was me I'd be the same. I'd be thinking poor man - of all the things to have happened. What's he going to do? How's he going to cope? I'd be exactly the same.

JIMMY
I thought post-mortems were held after the hand had been played.

VIC
Go on, Hugh. Pay no attention.

HUGH
What I'm trying to say is that it really isn't as bad as you probably think. In fact looked at in the cold light of day, what has happened could be positively beneficial.

ISOBEL
I'm sorry. You mean - you mean losing Mary?

VIC
Losing your wife could be beneficial?

JIMMY
Lovely. And now I think we have a misdeal. Count your hands, everybody.

EVERYONE automatically starts checking how many cards have been dealt to them as they continue.

HUGH
Of course - of course none of you will know what exactly happened, will you? And how it happened. And why should you when I didn't even know something was wrong.

ISOBEL
You had no idea?

HUGH
No not until it was too late, I'm afraid.

JIMMY
Misdeal. I've only got twelve cards. Misdeal.

JIMMY throws his cards down and the others follow suit, although HUGH is still counting his patiently.

HUGH
Yes. Yes I've got fourteen - so it is a misdeal.
(counting his cards)
No I really didn't know anything was wrong. Not until she had actually gone.

VIC
Until she had *gone?* You didn't know until Mary was *actually gone?*

HUGH
I hadn't a clue.

JIMMY
It's you to deal, Isabella.

ISOBEL gets handed the cards and starts to deal while VIC watches HUGH.

HUGH
How could I have known? Mary never said much. In this case she never said anything. She never gave the slightest indication anything was wrong.

ISOBEL
I can't believe there wasn't *some* sort of indication.

VIC
We were saying we both thought - the night Isobel came back from wherever - we both thought then that there might be something wrong with Mary.

HUGH
Really? More than I did.

ISOBEL
You mean all the time Mary was off somewhere -

HUGH
I just thought she was doing her thing. I never realised what was actually going on.

ISOBEL
Oh dear. Oh dear. Poor you.
(she puts a hand on his arm)
Poor Hugh. Poor you.

HUGH
But anyway. Anyway now it's all over and Mary's gone, I have to say all I can feel is the most enormous relief.

Which piece of information makes the dealer VIC drop some cards and look up in shock.

                              VIC
You what?

                            ISOBEL
                      (equally shocked)
You can't mean that.

                             HUGH
Believe me I've had plenty of time to think about it. And
once I sobered up and stopped feeling so damned sorry for
myself I realised what I felt. And that was a feeling of
overwhelming and unutterable relief.

ISOBEL looks at HUGH who looks back at her. VIC looks at
ISOBEL looking at HUGH who is looking at ISOBEL so VIC
then looks at JIMMY who looks back at her.

                            ISOBEL
You know this really is my fault, don't you?

                             HUGH
It's really got nothing to do with you whatsoever,
Isobel.

                            ISOBEL
It has, if you'll just listen. I think people had it
right before. Way back when. Before when you lost
somebody you went into mourning and that's where you
stayed. You stayed in mourning for two years. Three years
sometimes. Black first, then purple, then grey and then
white I think it was. Did you know that when the ancient
Egyptians lost a dog they went into mourning? Formal
mourning? The entire household. They covered everything
in black. All the statues of the other dogs and
everything in the entire household including their faces
would you believe? And that was just for their dog. And
in the days when we had to mourn properly we didn't go
gallivanting off to strange places with equally strange
people at the drop of a hat because we couldn't. It
wasn't done and it wasn't done for a very good reason.
You stayed where you were and in mourning until you came
back to your senses, which is exactly what we don't do
now, you see. And we should. We really still should. But
we're all in such a hurry. Such a tearing great hurry.
                           (pause)
And what happens is you run away from things. From
reality. I was running away. Running from the truth.
Trying to come to terms with something which I couldn't.
Certainly not in such a short space of time. And all I
ended up doing was making a complete tit of myself.

> VIC

No you're talking nonsense, Isadora. You did not make a *complete* tit of yourself.

> ISOBEL

Of course I did, Vic. I was a thoughtless and self-indulgent idiot. If I hadn't been I would never have met and run off with Alan - and none of this - none of this would ever have happened.

> HUGH
> (pause)

No we're talking about two very different things here, Isobel. And you can't be blamed for either of them or for anything. You'd lost Tom. Tom had died and you had lost your husband. Mary hasn't died. Mary isn't dead. Mary has simply fucked off.

> JIMMY

Careful. Ladies present.

> VIC

We're all grown-ups now, Jimmy. Thanks to Channel Four.

> HUGH

I'm sorry but that is exactly what Mary did I'm afraid. She simply and suddenly fucked off. It's the only way of putting it because that is exactly what the stupid girl did.

SILENCE. The TELEPHONE suddenly rings.

> JIMMY
> (counting his cards)

It's on answer.

It goes on RINGING.

> VIC

No it's bloody not.

> JIMMY

All right - so I forgot.

> VIC

So you go and bloody answer it then.

> JIMMY

The Ayatollah has spoken.
> (rising)

We got another misdeal anyway.

ISOBEL
That was my fault everyone. Sorry.

HUGH
(smiles ruefully)
I think the misdeal was actually my fault.

As JIMMY goes off to another room to answer the phone.

ISOBEL
Whatever you say the bastard Alan was down to me.

HUGH
No he wasn't, Isobel. He may have been a mistake - but he was your mistake. If Mary hadn't gone off with the bastard Alan she'd have gone off with some other bastard. One of her many, many and apparently countless and endless bastard admirers. I take it you did knew it was Alan?

ISOBEL
Yes.

VIC
We heard.

ISOBEL
Yes we knew it was Alan.

HUGH
Of course you did. Stupid of me. But you see if it hadn't been him it could and would have been someone else. It was only a question of time. Just a question of time. I'm only surprised she stayed as long as she did.

Silence.

VIC
Okay. Right. Well since this seems to be what they used to call a natural break, I think I'll go off and cut the half time sandwiches. Don't you move -
(putting a hand on ISOBEL'S shoulder)
You stay where you are and take care of Hugh.

HUGH
I do wish you'd stop fussing over me. I don't need taking care off.

VIC
Oh yes you do, pet. We all do.
(goes)

HUGH
You go back a long way you two, don't you?

ISOBEL
(with a glance at him)
We're not the only ones.
(picking up the discarded
cards and sorting them)

HUGH
How did you and Vic meet in the first place?

ISOBEL
Vic nursed my Dad in hospital. She was wonderful with him.

HUGH
Vic was a nurse?

ISOBEL
Yes. You don't know how Vic and Jimmy met?
(HUGH shakes his head)
She met Jimmy in York hospital. He wasn't sick - far from it. Although as it happens he very nearly died. His younger brother was very ill. He had Bright's disease, so Jimmy donated him one of his kidneys. Saved his brother's life. It's not a very pleasant experience apparently, giving someone one of your kidneys. Painful and dangerous too, even more so back then. Vic said she'd never met anyone like Jimmy. Always smiling, always cracking jokes. Never left his brother's side. Not for a moment. And even when Jimmy himself fell ill - he got some dreadful life threatening infection or other - he still didn't stop. Vic fell madly in love with him and has stayed there ever since. I know. I know sometimes it's hard to tell, but that's Vic. And that's Jimmy.

HUGH
All on one kidney.

ISOBEL
All his married life.

HUGH
Gosh.

ISOBEL
Gosh is right.

ISOBEL hands HUGH the pack of cards and HUGH looks at her. Then he takes them and carefully shuffles.

                    HUGH
The things we don't know.

                    ISOBEL
All we need to do is ask.

                    HUGH
All right. In that case is it okay if I ask you
something?
          (resetting the cards in the
           right place)
You don't have to answer it if you don't want to.

                    ISOBEL
All right. Fire ahead.

                    HUGH
When we were talking just now - and I said you'd
understand because you'd been through it too - only
through something infinitely worse - you said you didn't
necessarily agree. I don't see that. How?

                    ISOBEL
What I mean by that is that on some occasions infidelity
is even worse. It's like - it's like death without the
funeral. I think betrayal is one of the very worst thing
ever. Worse than anything. The constant lying and the
deceit. Then the discovery. It's the worst form of
treachery because it betrays the thing that matters most.
The heart.
          (beat)
I know because Tom was unfaithful.

Silence. HUGH stares at ISOBEL in disbelief. She moves a
deck of cards to the right of where VIC sits.

                    ISOBEL
                    (cont'd)
I think it must be Vic to deal. No Vic was dealing, so
it's you. You to deal.

                    HUGH
I just can't believe Tom was unfaithful. Vic said you
were the ideal couple.

                    ISOBEL
Once.
          (looks at him)
Look. Look when you're unfaithful you stop loving the
other person. You just can't love two people at the same
time. No matter what anyone says.

HUGH
Did you stop loving Tom?

ISOBEL
Not for a moment. Because I didn't know.

HUGH
But you found out.

ISOBEL
Only after he had died.

HUGH looks at her, appalled.

ISOBEL
I got a telephone call.
          (almost wearily)
From his mistress. His girl friend. Whatever you like to call her. I got a telephone call.

HUGH
Heavens. I see. No wonder you were so - you were at such a loss.

ISOBEL
I was at a loss all right. So much so that on one or two occasions I actually thought I'd -
          (stops)
I'm fine now. Much better. It isn't that I've accepted it. Or drawn a line under it. Or put it behind me and moved on. On the contrary. I haven't done any of these things. I've simply recognised it. Recognised that it happened, that there's nothing I can do about it, and most of all I have recognised the fact that right up to the day Tom died I loved him.

HUGH
But if you'd known -

ISOBEL
But I didn't. I didn't know.

HUGH
I didn't know either. About Mary. About her proclivity. About exactly what she was up to. But the difference between you and I - the big difference in our situation is I didn't love Mary.

ISOBEL looks at him long and hard with a frown, in silence.

ISOBEL
I was under the impression you were mad about her. We all were.

HUGH
I thought I was. Initially I was very attracted to her - very much so. Mary's a very attractive woman, Isobel, believe me. And when she turns those headlights on - oh boy. But I was never in love with her, and when I found out, I suppose I felt guilty. Which is why I indulged her. Gave her her head. Let her do and say more or less as she chose. I loved Catherine, you see. My first wife. Cathy was the one I really loved and then when Cathy - when Cathy bolted - which she did - I span - and when I was spinning enter Mary. When you're spinning you get dizzy, and when you're dizzy you can't see properly.

ISOBEL
No. You're right. You most certainly can't.

THEY fall to SILENCE.

HUGH
Wonder where the other two have got to.

ISOBEL
Yes. Yes I wonder.

HUGH
Shall I go and see?

ISOBEL
No. Because now it's my turn. It's my turn to ask you something. And again - you don't have to answer.

HUGH
Fine. Go ahead. And I swear to tell the truth - the whole truth and nothing but the truth.

ISOBEL
Where were you on St. Valentine's night thirty nine years ago?

HUGH
Thirty nine years ago? Is it really that long ago?

ISOBEL
Where did you get to?

HUGH
I was where I said I'd be. Where were you?

ISOBEL
I was where I said I'd be. Where you told me to be.

HUGH
You were not. Because I was there and you most certainly were not.

ISOBEL
Oh yes I was. You can ask the waiters. They felt so sorry for me they bought me champagne.

HUGH
Sweetheart. You were not there. I was there - I was there in Carlo One

ISOBEL
Carlo One?

HUGH
I was there for two and a half hours and you were most definitely not there.

ISOBEL
We'd agreed to meet in Carlo Two. Which was where I was.

HUGH
Carlo Two? No. I think we had agreed to meet in Carlo One.

ISOBEL
No we hadn't. I think we'd agreed to meet in Carlo Two.

HUGH
Oh Christ.
        (quietly, looking at her)
Christ I thought you'd stood me up.

ISOBEL
I thought you'd stood me up.

HUGH
Stand you up? Why should I stand you up? I even had the ring.

ISOBEL
You had what?

HUGH
Never mind.

ISOBEL
You had *what?*

HUGH
I said - never mind.

ISOBEL
Never mind? How could I not mind!

HUGH
You didn't mind enough to turn up in the right place!

ISOBEL
I thought I'd gone to the right place! So even if you had, how was I to know? All I knew was that you weren't there! Where we'd arranged to meet! Why didn't you ring me? You should have rung me! Why didn't you call the next day and ask me where I was?

HUGH
(standing)
Why do you think? Because I thought you'd stood me up! And men don't like being stood up!

ISOBEL
(standing)
Why on earth did you think I'd stood you up?

HUGH
Because you weren't bloody well there, that's why! You could have rung me!

ISOBEL
That's not something girls did then! Don't be stupid!

HUGH
I am not being stupid! And as it happened I did ring you. A couple of days after. I rang and left a message with your mother!

ISOBEL
With my mother? No wonder I didn't get it! You left a message with my mother? You know what she felt about you! My mother hated lawyers! Ever since my father and she got divorced - oh it doesn't matter. You were the last person she wanted me to marry so she was the last person you should have left a message with.

HUGH
I didn't know that! Not at the time. I rang up to speak to you and your mother promised she'd pass the message on.

ISOBEL
Well she didn't.

HUGH
So I gather. So when you didn't ring back naturally I assumed -

ISOBEL
You shouldn't ever assume anything. And there's really no need to look quite so tragic.

HUGH
There is every need. Every need. Just think, for God's sake, Isobel. Just think! God Almighty! Jesus Christ!

HUGH collapses back on to his chair. At this point VIC backs in from the kitchen, carrying plates of sandwiches.

VIC
What's all the shouting about? I hope you haven't started playing without me.

HUGH
You're not going to believe this.

ISOBEL
It's not really any of Vic's business.

VIC
All the more reason you should tell me. You know how I thrive on what's not my business.

HUGH
You will never believe this.

ISOBEL
Thirty nine years ago Hugh asked me to meet him for dinner and thought I'd stood him up.

HUGH
She only went to wrong restaurant.

ISOBEL
There were two restaurants both with the same name -

HUGH
They did not both have the same name, Isobel! One was called Carlo One and the other was called Carlo Two.

VIC
I'd call that the same name. Give or take a one and a two.

ISOBEL
Why on earth would I stand you up, Hugh? Think about it. I said I'd wait until you'd finished your articles and I did - I waited all that time so why on earth would I stand you up after waiting that long?

HUGH
I don't know! What was I supposed to think?

VIC
Hello hello.
    (putting down her sandwiches)
This has the distinct ring of a lover's tiff.

HUGH and ISOBEL fall silent like children discovered.

VIC
You don't mean it?
    (grins)
Well I'll be bugger-red.
    (sic)

HUGH
I even had the ring.

VIC
Well I'll be double bugger-red. You don't mean to say you two were an item?

ISOBEL
They didn't have that expression then.

VIC
All right. So were you courting?

HUGH
We were indeed an item, Vic. Even if then there was no such a thing.

HUGH takes his wallet out and from it produces an ancient strip of booth photos.

HUGH
Taken in the photo booth on Victoria Station.

ISOBEL
    (looks at him)
What's that. Let me see.

HUGH
Thirty nine years ago.

ISOBEL
You still have them?

HUGH
Of course I still have them.

ISOBEL
You carry them round with you?

HUGH
Yes. Yes I carry them around with me. Everywhere.

VIC
Give us a butcher's.
(looking at the photos)
That's never you two. Is it? Will you just look at you. Just look at the two of you.

VIC shows ISOBEL the photos. At first ISOBEL is reluctant to look, then gives in.

ISOBEL
Gracious heavens.

HUGH
Wasn't Isobel pretty?

VIC
What are you talking about? She still is.

HUGH
No she isn't. Now she's beautiful.

ISOBEL
Now you're being ridiculous.

HUGH
(looking at the photo)
How I loved you in that frock.

VIC
Now there's a word you don't hear very often these days.

ISOBEL
Frock?

VIC
Love.

HUGH
I still can't look at gingham. Particularly red and white gingham

                    ISOBEL
I got it at Fenwicks. In the Sale.

                    VIC
          (taking the photos back)
I used to have my hair in bunches. *And* with matching
ribbons.

                    HUGH
Matching gingham ribbons.

                    VIC
The two of you. Fancy that. Thirty nine years ago.

                    HUGH
I can remember that day like it was yesterday.

                    ISOBEL
We were just off to Brighton. First class on the Pullman.
The Brighton Pullman. It was a really lovely spring day -
rather windy on the beach. The spray came off the waves
and stung our faces and our eyes. We walked on the beach
and you took photographs then we walked to the pier where
we shot the shark -

                    VIC
You shot a shark?

                    ISOBEL
It was an arcade game. Became a favourite. Shooting the
Shark. We shot the shark then we went and had lunch in a
little fish bar in a side street. We had fresh Brighton
prawns in cream and fish and chips. Best fish and chips
I've ever eaten. It was a magic day. I've always
remembered that magic day. It's the sort of day you keep
in a very special frame.

                    HUGH
It's the sort of day no one ever forgets.

                    VIC
And just think what might have happened if you hadn't
both gone to the wrong restaurant.

                    HUGH
We didn't *both* go to the wrong restaurant, Vic.

                    VIC
Can you imagine.
          (regards them both)
I wonder what would have happened.

HUGH
Yes I wonder.

ISOBEL
I don't.

She looks at him and they get caught up in the look.

VIC
Talking of which - about wondering - anyone seen Jimmy? He can't still be on the telephone. He hates the telephone. Jimmy? Jimmy? *Jimmy* -

It seems as if JIMMY is not going to reappear then just as VIC becomes visibly anxious and is moving to the study door JIMMY re-enters.

JIMMY
I go. I come back. Right. Bet you don't know who said that. I go I come back.

VIC
No and I couldn't give a flying freehold either. Just don't do that.

JIMMY
Just don't do what, my love?

VIC
Don't go disappearing like that. You gave me a fright.

JIMMY
I was on the *phone,* petal. Not having a heart attack. Now back to the table, children.

VIC
All right, all right - but before we do - you just wait till you hear what's been going on out here.

JIMMY
I heard. Every word. Come on - to table.

VIC
You were eavesdropping?

JIMMY
I was being tactful. I didn't want to interrupt our love birds here so I waited till they were done. Or till you barged in rather.
            (moving to table)
Anyone remember whose deal was it?

ISOBEL
I think it might be Hugh's.

VIC
No it isn.t, It's me.

JIMMY
Right. So come on then, Gladys -

VIC holds JIMMY back by his arm as the other two go back to the table.

VIC
Who was it on the phone? Or shouldn't I ask.

JIMMY
That depends on what you want to hear. It was the daughter.

VIC
Thought it might be. What did she want?

JIMMY
Guess. She has - apparently - in her words - maxed her credit card.

VIC
Again?

JIMMY
Again.

VIC
(cautiously)
So what did you tell her?

JIMMY
I told her sorry. Said sorry but the party's over, pet. The candles have flickered and dimmed, the sock is empty and the piggy bank's in receivership.

VIC
You never did. You never.

JIMMY
Time someone did.

VIC
Was it just money she wanted? Sure there wasn't anything else?

JIMMY
Anything else.
          (pause)
I nearly forgot. The painting. But I was right. It isn't
by who you thought it was.

VIC
Oh. Oh isn't it?

JIMMY
'Fraid not, petal. Afraid not. I was right and thou were
wrong.

VIC
Oh. All right. Okay. Fair enough. And that was it, was
it? That was all she said?

JIMMY
That was it. All except to tell you apparently the
painting's by someone altogether different. Don't ask me
who. I wrote the name of the artist down for you. You
know me and names. Here.

JIMMY gives her a folded piece of paper.

JIMMY
          (generally)
Come on - table everyone.

VIC stands with the piece of paper in her hand, still
folded, not ready to read it yet.

HUGH
Isobel, dearest - cut to Vic, will you?

ISOBEL does so.

JIMMY
Bless these cards oh Lord I pray - Victoria? It's you to
deal, Blossom -

But VIC is not ready yet. JIMMY sighs.

JIMMY
Deal for her, Hugh. Or we'll be here all year.

HUGH deals quickly and expertly. With her back to them
VIC slowly opens the folded piece of paper and taking her
glasses off the top of her head she prepares to read it.
The others are already picking up their hands and sorting
them.

JIMMY
(looking at his cards)
Gollox.
(mock gloomy)
No bid.

ISOBEL
One heart.

VIC is still standing. She now reads the paper.

JIMMY
Victoria?

VIC
In a moment.

JIMMY
(sorting his cards)
We're all waiting for you, Victoria.

VIC
Bloody hell.
(quietly as she reads)
Blazes Kate. Bloody hell fire.

She folds the paper again and comes to sit. No one has picked up on what she said except perhaps JIMMY who glances at her. VIC folds the paper up and puts it beside her. She picks up her hand and starts to sort it. Silence.

VIC
Sorry. No bid.

HUGH
Three hearts.

JIMMY
No.

VIC
(looking at JIMMY)
You sure, Jimmy? You sure about this?

JIMMY
That is the message she gave. That apparently is what the man said.

VIC
Bloody hell fire.

JIMMY
Quiet.

HUGH
Bloody hell fire?
(to ISOBEL)
I suspect they're using some sort of new convention, don't you?

ISOBEL
Sounds very much like it to me.

VIC
You absolutely sure, Jimbo?

JIMMY
Sure as eggs are high in cholesterol. It's you to bid, Isabella.

ISOBEL
Four hearts.

JIMMY
Just like that.

VIC
No.

HUGH
No.

JIMMY
No.

ISOBEL
Four hearts it is then.

VIC unfolds the piece of paper and reads it again unnoticed by ISOBEL and HUGH who are busy studying their hands.

JIMMY
And they are your hearts, my love. And may God bless all who sail in you.

VIC looks once more again to check the piece of paper and then across at JIMMY. She gives him a look. He smiles lovingly back at her. VIC smiles in return then shakes her head in disbelief. But the smile stays right on her face.

VIC leads a card, HUGH lays down his hand as dummy.

                        ISOBEL
                   (looking at dummy)
Thank you, partner.

ISOBEL pulls dummy's hand towards her and looks at it
very carefully.

                        ISOBEL
In fact thank you very much indeed. And you know
something? I think that this time we might just make it.

                        HUGH
My thoughts entirely. In fact I think we stand a very
good chance. Partner.

ISOBEL glances across at him and HUGH smiles back at her
and keeps smiling as he sits back and happily folds his
arms. ISOBEL plays a card from dummy, JIMMY plays and
ISOBEL wins the trick. She leads her next card and VIC
plays. ISOBEL plays quickly and confidently from dummy,
JIMMY chucks down a card and ISOBEL wins the second
trick. VIC opens her piece of paper for the last time,
reads it and smiles again at JIMMY who mouths her a kiss
in return.

A burst of late autumn sunshine floods the room as the
FOUR friends play out the hand and

                    THE CURTAIN FALLS

Printed in Great Britain
by Amazon